An introduction to social work
A PRIMER

BETTY J. PICCARD
School of Social Work
The Florida State University

1975

The Dorsey Press   *Homewood, Illinois   60430*
Irwin-Dorsey International   London, England   WC2H 9NJ
Irwin-Dorsey Limited   Georgetown, Ontario   L7G 4B3

First Printing, February 1975

ISBN 0-256-01738-7
Library of Congress Catalog Card No. 74–27540
Printed in the United States of America

Foreword

Experiments begun in the 1960s have culminated in revolutionary changes for social work education in the 1970s. The bachelor's degree in social work has been recognized as the appropriate credential for beginning social work practice. Until 1971 professional membership in the National Association of Social Workers was limited to those holding a Master's of Social Work. Many influences contributed to change this pattern which had been established and had prevailed for some 50 years. Increased demand for personnel with varying levels of competence to participate in the expanded service delivery system; improved education at the secondary level; introduction of more sophisticated and efficient learning technologies; increased cost of higher education; telescoping of the educational process; new career opportunities; and changes in standards for professional membership in the association served to move us in the direction of establishing a new entry level for the profession. The factors enumerated represent a restrictive rather than an exhaustive review of the pressures which led to change. Suffice it to say that the shift reflected demands perceived from within the profession as well as those imposed by alterations occurring in the broader society. The amount of time spent in acquiring an education has become less significant than the competence achieved.

The traditional two year graduate program has been reconceptualized to encompass an educational continuum. This requires the establishment of basic or minimal expectations for certifying professional competence as well as mastery. The essential knowledge and skill components comprising such qualifications are presently under careful professional scrutiny. Betty Piccard's book is the result of such an attempt to factor out baseline knowledge for beginning direct practice.

Years of professional experience combined with supervising social work interns, followed by teaching generic methodology at both the undergraduate and graduate levels have provided the background and perspective for Piccard's work. The selection of content which includes underlying philosophy and values plus a brief historical overview presents substantive information about the major interventive technologies within the theoretical framework of social systems. This considerable task has been accomplished in highly readable form offering both primary content and a solid foundation for advanced professional education. The development of materials for differential professional preparation is essential within the current reformulation of social work education. Piccard's book represents a significant contribution directed toward this end of providing educators and students with a sound beginning text.

L. Diane Bernard, Ph.D.
Dean, School of Social Work
Florida State University
Tallahassee, Florida

Preface

This book aims to give a picture of basic issues in social work policy and practice. It does not attempt to cover all the issues, but rather to indicate some of the change and ferment that are current in social work thinking and behavior. While the organization follows the traditional classification of the main methods of casework, group work, and community work, commonalities as well as differences in these methods will be pointed out.

The need for a basic preliminary text is evident. As more programs in undergraduate social work come into being, the need will become more obvious. The traditional texts, used by graduate students, are too specific and too long to be read in one term by beginning students. The aim of this text is to provide essential reading material for one term; it presents beginning ideas about the three fields of direct service, as well as a frame of reference that consists of a central value orientation coupled with systems concepts. In this text historical discussion is kept at a minimum in order to spend more time on current practice and future trends.

Beginning students need an organizing framework as a guide to future practice. Systems theory, with its implications for input, processing, output, and feedback, seems to provide that framework. It is used throughout this text in combination with planned-change theory and introductions to various modes of intervention. This approach is used in describing social work roles and tasks in relation to each of the methods, as well as to common features of all the methods.

In the past, preparation for the profession of social work has been at the graduate level. Persons who have achieved the degree of Master of Social Work have been sought after as helpers with individual, group, and community problems. Their knowledge, skills, and values have been needed in mental health work, veterans' administration, adoption agencies, juvenile courts, and hospitals, to mention only a few of the many settings in which social workers have been active. They have worked with individuals, groups, and organizations; they have worked directly with clients and have helped indirectly to provide services as planners and administrators. The assumption has been that social workers have had a four year degree, probably in the liberal arts, and an additional two years of professional education, including field work. For many years the assumption always has been that there are not and never will be enough social workers to meet the ever increasing needs.

With the advent of the war on poverty during the 1960s, some new ideas concerning helping roles were tried out in practice. Indigenous workers, case aides, and student workers were able to work with and under professional workers. In some cases the experiment worked better than in others. But the gap between professional and nonprofessional had been breached.

Undergraduate programs in social work, both in lower and upper division colleges, have been expanding to meet this increased demand. The demand comes from employers who see a semiprofessional worker as better than no professional help at all, and from students who see the field of social work as an attractive substitute for the more abstract "hard sciences."

Unfortunately, the literature in the field has not kept up with the increasing demand for undergraduate courses in social work. Journals that present articles about social casework, group work, and community work are still directed toward the highly educated professional. This book is intended to help close this gap in our current literature.

This book was written in Tallahassee and in London during 1973 and 1974, but the philosophy and foundations have been developing over the past quarter century, and represent the results of interaction with professors, colleagues, clients, and students over that period. I am grateful to all of them. Particularly, I appreciate the support of Dean

Diane Bernard of the Florida State University School of Social Work, who read the entire manuscript and made helpful suggestions. In the actual writing, I have received tremendous support, both moral and substantive from my husband, Paul, who wields a wicked editing pencil, from my daughter, Jane, a recently graduated Master of Social Work, and from my other children, Mary and Ann, Bob and John, all of whom have read portions of the text and made suggestions for additions or deletions.

Reviewers Robin M. Williams, Consulting Editor, Sheldon R. Gelman, Gwendolyn C. Gilbert, John M. Herrick, and Ronda S. Connaway have given suggestions and recommendations for revision and reworking. I appreciate all their help. Finally, I am grateful to Patti Terrie, Guy Spearman, Phyllis Cloman and Mara Harmon, all of whom typed and retyped portions of the manuscript.

January 1975   **Betty J. Piccard**

Contents

1

Social work philosophy and values

The terms *social welfare, public welfare,* and *social work* seem to require some defining. Wilensky and Lebaux, in *Industrial Society and Social Welfare* have defined social welfare in two ways: as residual and institutional.

> Two conceptions of social welfare seem to be dominant in the United States today: the *residual* and the *institutional.* The first holds that social welfare institutions should come into play only when the normal structures of supply, the family and the market break down. The second, in contrast, sees the welfare services as normal, "first line" functions of modern industrial society. These are the concepts around which drives for more or less welfare service tend to focus. Not surprisingly, they derive from the ethos of the society in which they are found. They represent a compromise between the values of economic individualism and free enterprise on the one hand, and security, equality, and humanitarianism on the other. They are rather explicit among both social welfare professionals and the lay public.[1]

The first conception describes institutions which come into play only when normal structures such as the family and the job market break down. The second sees "welfare" as a normal function of modern society. For our purpose, we may accept the second conception as "social welfare" and the first as "public welfare."

---

[1] Wilensky, Harold L., and Lebeaux, Charles N., *Industrial Society and Social Welfare* (New York: Free Press, Publication of the Russell Sage Foundation, 1965), p. 138.

Social welfare, public welfare and social work

Social welfare involves all the functions performed by society to meet the needs of all the people in the society. Institutions such as schools, highways and post offices are included, as well as social security, public assistance and health insurance.

Public welfare is the system which supplies certain goods and services to certain people whose normal sources of supply have broken down. Families without a wage earner, the aged and aging, and the handicapped, are examples of people who might be unable to meet their own needs.

With such simple, rational definitions, how can there be so many and such strong feelings about the whole concept of welfare? The answer is that rational definitions do not determine feelings. An interesting experiment is to ask families, friends or casual acquaintances for a brief rational explanation of the terms in question.

Richard Titmuss, noted British economist, is one authority who suggests that public welfare ought not to be differentiated from social welfare. He suggests that the two are the same. Programs, whether public or private, which are designed for the welfare of any group benefit other groups as well. In his view, most of the money spent in public welfare is spent on middle- or upper-class people. If we look at public programs in the United States, we see that the Veterans' Administration and Social Security programs are tax-funded programs, most of whose provisions benefit groups other than the very poor. Furthermore, we must recognize that various types of tax "breaks" involving great sums of money are available only to the very rich.

For the most part, social work as a profession, and social workers as individuals, tend to agree with Titmuss and to see welfare as an all-inclusive function of society today. While many social workers are involved with the residual aspects of meeting emergency situations by providing goods and services where there has been a breakdown, many others work as planners, educators and administrators concerned with the broader aspect of welfare.

While social workers might see tax breaks for the wealthy as less worthwhile uses of public funds, they subscribe to the proposition that public support for any given group has an effect on all groups. If there is only a limited amount to be spent, it should be spent for those whose need is greatest. Social workers see the importance of looking at large complex systems, trying to see the relationships between systems, and of planning for the best use of goods and resources.

For many people in our society, the word "welfare" has strong emotional connotations. To a recipient of public assistance, "the welfare" may be seen as an all-powerful monolithic organization wielding life and death power. To a taxpayer struggling to keep up with increasing living costs, welfare may mean "no-good deadbeats getting something for nothing." To a semanticist, the word may mean simply faring well, a state of well-being. It is clear that neat, tidy definitions do not adequately explain the kinds of conflicts that may be elicited by any mention of social welfare or public welfare.

Questionnaire

Answering the following questionnaire may give you some idea of where you stand with respect to the residual-institutional dichotomy, as well as an idea about your attitudes toward welfare and social workers. Do you agree or disagree with the following statements?

1. Welfare recipients are mainly people who are too lazy to work.
2. Illegitimacy is encouraged by the practice of increasing the amount of the grant according to the number of children.
3. Receiving public assistance runs in the family.
4. Welfare recipients receive all necessary medical care free of charge.
5. Social workers should be very careful not to pamper applicants for public assistance.
6. Most social work is done by psychiatric social workers.
7. Mentally ill people are nearly always best cared for in mental institutions.
8. The trend in the treatment of juvenile delinquency is toward more permissiveness.
9. A social worker's main job is giving people advice.
10. The idea of helping people to help themselves assumes a degree of competence in welfare recipients which most do not have.
11. The use of groups by social workers is a fad which will probably die out soon.

12. If you had a serious problem, you would probably think of asking for help from a psychiatrist rather than a social worker.
13. Policemen cannot use social work methods because they deal with a different type person.
14. If a person under the influence of alcohol asks for help, a social worker should always refer him to another agency.
15. If a person admits using drugs, a social worker should always refer him to the police.
16. Persons who are having marital problems would probably rather talk with a psychologist than with a social worker.
17. To say that a social worker helps people to help themselves means that he knows what is best for them and helps them to get it.
18. Social workers should work for the satisfaction of helping others without pay.

These questions, your answers and discussions around them may help to clarify some basic issues and facts in social work.

Knowledge, skills, values

Harriett Bartlett, in her article on "Social Work Practice" in the *Encyclopedia of Social Work* says:

> Social work practice is recognized by a constellation of value, purpose, knowledge and interventive techniques. Some social work practice shows more extensive use of one or the other of the components, but it is a social work practice only when they are all present to some degree.[2]

These attributes are necessary for a social worker, then: knowledge, skills, purpose and values.

Knowledge of human behavior has developed rapidly in the last 70 years. We recognize now—since Freud's initial work—that many factors affect an individual, and that even more factors affect groups and communities. Human development from birth to death is an important facet of the knowledge we need, but it is only one facet. The old argument about the influence of heredity versus environment[3] requires broadening and deepening. It is impossible to predict future behavior

---

[2] Bartlett, Harriett, "Social Work Practice," *Encyclopedia of Social Work,* 16 (New York: National Association of Social Workers, 1970), 1479.

[3] Goddard, H. H., *Feeblemindedness: Its Causes and Consequences* (New York: Macmillan, 1914).

simply by a knowledge of genetic, prenatal, infantile and early child-hood history. We think that an individual begins life as a unique being whose family, growth pattern and other stimuli have some effect, but we are no longer likely to predict a simple cause-effect relationship, no matter how much we know about an individual's past.

We know, too, that people behave differently in their own families than they do with their friends; differently with strangers; and still differently in large organizations and in communities. Social work skills have developed as we have gained knowledge about different kinds of behavior in different kinds of settings.

Somewhat belatedly we have come to recognize that people from minority social, ethnic, and cultural backgrounds react differently when they relate with people and situations from the majority culture. We have learned that the majority view of our society is not the only one, or even necessarily the best one. The term *institutional racism* refers to one form of social inconsistency, inequity and injustice with which we have had to become familiar and knowledgeable.

Casework skills have developed as a result of our efforts to help individuals as individuals on a one-to-one basis, using either a problem-solving[4] or a psychosocial approach.[5] Many social workers spend most of their time practicing casework. Psychiatric social workers, medical social workers, school social workers, delinquency and adoption work-ers all have regarded individual casework as their primary area of special skill. Group work, however, has also moved into all these areas as workers have acquired more knowledge about the importance of groups to individuals at every age. People in like circumstances can help each other, confront each other and understand each other.

In the past ten years, family therapy has become a special kind of social work as a result of work done by such family therapy experts as Nathan Ackerman, Virginia Satir, Don Jackson and others. These peo-ple feel very strongly that treating the individual alone will not solve the problem. Only through observing the family members as they inter-act with each other can the worker learn what is wrong and how to help the family change it.[6]

---

[4] Perlman, Helen H., *Social Casework: A Problem-Solving Process*, 12th ed. (Chicago: University of Chicago Press, 1967).

[5] Hollis, Florence, *Casework: A Psycho-Social Therapy*, 6th ed. (New York: Random House, 1966).

[6] Satir, Virginia, *Conjoint Family Therapy* (Palo Alto, Calif.: Science and Be-havior Books, 1967).

Caseworkers, group workers and family workers have all learned from each other. They have also learned that they need to work with larger groups, with communities and organizations. This requires still other skills and still different knowledge as well as new applications of existing skills and knowledge. For example, a caseworker may have several clients who have the same problem—for instance, drug abuse, with its many ramifications. Perhaps an encounter group is called for so that the clients can help each other. In addition, other persons in the community should be made aware of the extent of the problem and some of the possible alternatives available to prevent or modify it. Another example might be that of a caseworker in a welfare agency who knows that many clients are concerned about the poor service given by slum landlords. The complaint of one tenant can be brushed off but complaints from a group may carry weight. The caseworker may thus feel that organizing a tenants' group for social action will be an important kind of help for each individual tenant. It is plain that all social workers need some skills in all three areas of social work.

Social work values

Because social work has been so concerned with values, it may be well to consider some of these values. Lists of social work values and the principles developed from them have proliferated, but the areas of agreement, not those of disagreement, stand out. Perhaps one of the best known and most widely accepted of the lists is Biestek's principles of the casework relationship.[7] The relationship between professional worker and clients is an important factor in all kinds of social work. These principles are applicable to all kinds of relationships in the social work profession. They are:

1. *Individualization.* Every individual, group, and community is unique and deserving of consideration as such. Each individual has dignity and worth, on his or her own merits. A person can never be viewed as one of the mob. By the same token, every social worker is an individual who knows and understands himself or herself, uses his or her own attributes and talents to the best of individual ability and to the clients' best good as that can be determined.

The social worker's skills and knowledge are used in the context of

---

[7] Biestek, Felix P., *The Casework Relationship* (Chicago: Loyola University Press, 1957).

the worker's own personality. If a beginning social worker has rather sketchy self-knowledge and understanding, at least he or she recognizes the need to improve these, and works in that direction. It is to be hoped that as other kinds of knowledge and skill are gained, the worker will improve in self-knowledge and skill because he or she will be trying to do so.

For example, a student worker was working with a mother of three young children, who was looking vainly for work. She was unskilled and had no satisfactory day care plans for her children. The worker made various suggestions about factory work, waitress work, and sales. When she reported her efforts to the supervisor, the supervisor suggested the possibility of AFDC. The student was aghast at the thought of an able-bodied young woman "going on welfare." When she thought more about it she realized that employment was unlikely and apt to be unsatisfactory, and she concluded that her initial reaction reflected her upbringing, rather than her judgment about the propriety of welfare. In this example, the student learned something about herself, but she also learned something about the community resources and something about the needs and resources of this individual client.

2. *Purposeful expression of feeling.* Every individual, every group, every community has the need to express their feelings. Their right to do so is basic to social work. Emotions are as important as thoughts or beliefs or knowledge, and negative emotions are as important as positive emotions.

The leader of a group of delinquent boys noted that the group was asking fairly hostile questions of him. He accepted one member's explanation that they were tired of all these meetings, and listened to their complaints about the group's progress. Then he reviewed again the limitations placed by the court on the group, giving the boys a full explanation of the details. The group leader allowed the members to express their hostility, because they needed to vent their feelings. But he put realistic limits on the group because they needed to be reminded of them, also. His aim was support with limits.

3. *Controlled emotional involvement.* Every individual, every group, every community has a right to expect that someone will be able to relate to their level of feeling. A social worker must be able to *feel* with another, not just talk with him. The worker need not *have* the same feelings, but he or she must show understanding of the feelings of the other person.

Mrs. Black recounted with tears in her eyes, just how her husband had died. When she finished, she began to cry softly. Her caseworker responded by putting her hand on her shoulder without speaking. The caseworker was involved, sympathetic, responsive. She was not asked for and did not give advice. She showed nonverbally her concern.

4. *Acceptance.* Every individual, every group and every community has a right to be accepted for what they are, not what the social worker wishes they were. The social worker tries to understand where they are at this moment, and to work from there. This is not the same as saying that the social worker approves of everything the client does.

Mrs. Brown has been arrested, at the instigation of a neighbor, for beating her two-year-old child. The court social worker greeted her sympathetically and asked if she would like to have someone to talk with. Mrs. Brown nodded gratefully. Without approving the client's behavior, the worker was able to indicate acceptance of Mrs. Brown as a person.

5. *Nonjudgmental attitude.* This precludes assigning guilt or innocence, and regards "blame" as outside the social worker's function. The whole question of whether a person is worthy or unworthy of help seems a quaint anomaly to most social workers, though many people continue to feel that moral judgments must be made.

Carrie Smith was not an attractive client. An acknowledged prostitute, she had come to the public health clinic for counseling on family planning, but suggested that she might have been exposed to syphilis. The medical social worker arranged for her to see the health officer immediately and assured Carrie that she had done the right thing to come to the clinic.

6. *Self-determination.* This is one of the most difficult things to give a client. Workers who are asked for help must give help and advice, but just as surely every client has a right to use or reject help, to take advice or to reject it. The client has the ownership of his problems. The concepts of individualization and acceptance include a recognition of the individual's right to self-determination.

A tenants' organization whose efforts to see the landlord had been unsuccessful, suggested to their worker that they try picketing the landlord's home. The worker sympathized with their frustration but suggested that the landlord's neighbors might be unsympathetic and suggested an alternative action, which he would lead. The tenants were not interested and went ahead with their picketing plan.

7. *Confidentiality.* Finally, every client has a right to expect confidences to be kept. Every client should be able to take for granted that

discussions with a social worker will not be the subject of later gossip sessions. Workers can and do discuss their clients with their supervisors —to learn how best to help—but they cannot and should not discuss their clients freely with others. In several states bills are now under consideration, which would give social workers the same kind of immunity to legal action as that enjoyed by doctors and lawyers in protecting the confidences they receive.

All of these concepts are necessary with any size client system to form and maintain a satisfactory social work relationship. Biestek was thinking of relationships with individuals, but relationships with groups and communities require that the same principles be followed.

Important as these seven concepts and the values they represent are, however, they all produce their corollary value dilemmas. In individualizing, workers must recognize that generalization has a place in social work thinking. Human beings grow and develop at similar rates, and behavior which is acceptable at one age is neither acceptable nor normal at a later age. Also, cultural norms are different in different places and at different times. This is glaringly true in poverty and ghetto cultures where children must learn at a very early age to protect themselves from a whole variety of dangers, to care for younger siblings, and to master a whole spectrum of important, responsible behaviors.

When does purposeful expression of feeling lose its purpose? The idea that everyone has a right to feelings, and that feelings play a large part in dealing with any kind of problem, must be tempered with the opposite idea that feeling in large doses can hinder both worker and client. Social workers have had to deal with their public image as "bleeding hearts and do-gooders" not because of controlled emotional responses, but because of uncontrolled emotional responses. Their emphasis on human feelings has left social workers open to criticism from those who emphasize facts and figures.

The acceptance of the worker who extended sympathy to Mrs. Brown might be construed as acceptance of child beating. Clearly, acceptance and a nonjudgmental attitude are not only difficult to practice, but are also open to a great deal of question from within and without the profession. How can people have values without questioning those who have different values?

Perhaps the most difficult value to maintain and to justify is that of self-determination. Can social workers really let people decide for themselves how to bring up their children, when their ways may be harmful to those children? Can social workers really allow would-be suicides self-determination? Do people really have a right to decide whether or not they should live on public assistance or work for less than a living wage? Are social workers really in a position to protect people, to do for them, to make decisions for them? Perhaps this value too, is open to question and qualification.

Finally, the value of confidentiality may be questioned. If welfare is right, if clients are to be encouraged to seek help with problems, why is it necessary to keep their efforts and our response to those efforts a secret? Donald Howard, in *Social Welfare: Values, Means, and Ends* says:

> The penchant of welfare agencies to treat as confidential all transactions with beneficiaries reflects an inimical view of the need to be helped and of being helped. If this were not the case, one would expect a family service agency, for instance, not to cloak in secrecy but to divulge as a mark of honor the news that a particular family had applied to it for help or having been helped, was now functioning happily. However, resort to family service—or any other welfare service—is seldom thought to characterize "The Family of Distinction" in the sense that drinking a particular mineral water, smoking a certain brand of cigar, or using some other prestigious product is alleged to mark the "Man of Distinction."[8]

Summary

Social welfare, social work, social intervention, and public welfare are separate entities, though connected by a common philosophy. Concern for other people has been a traditional basis for the practice of social work. Social workers need knowledge and skills, as well as values. Their knowledge must encompass the areas of human and organizational behavior, of social policy, of social research, and of methods of practice. Skills in social work have included casework, which is social work with individuals, group work, which is social work with groups, and community work, which is social work with larger communities. All three skills assume an understanding of some principles of relationship. The character of the helping relationship is considered an important common factor in all types of social work.

---

[8] Howard, Donald, *Social Welfare: Values, Means, and Ends* (New York: Random House, 1969), p. 193.

2

Social systems

We hear a great deal these days about "the system," about living with it, about beating it. The term system means a great many things to a great many people. Natural scientists have always referred to solar systems, biologists to circulatory systems, and political scientists to capitalist or communist systems. The most recent use of the term is in computer terminology, where it is used to describe complex mechanical processes. Computers accept input of data, process it, and turn out other data or output.

The concept is useful to social workers because it provides a way of seeing relationships in time and space between ideas and things. Particularly, it is useful to see the relationships between individuals, with whom social workers are concerned, in whatever role social workers take.

What is a system?

We have two problems with the concept of systems: first, defining our own use of the word, and second, and more important, describing the existing systems that influence and are influenced by social workers. When we call something "a system" or "the system," what are we saying about it? Our label conveys our perception of a process, a variety of shifting relationships, a transformation, some influences,

11

some results and boundaries. In our vocabulary, then, *system* means a set of dynamic general relationships which together process stimuli (inputs) through a subsystem of closer relationships, thereby producing responses (outputs). Model systems can be seen in the organic parts of an individual, in an individual taken as a whole, and in groups of individuals ranging in size from pairs to billions.

For example, humans have a blood circulation system. Nerve signals resulting from emotions, fatigue, and so forth, and blood come to the heart and lungs (the subset of closer relationships), where the blood is transformed and sent on its way again until it reaches the outer boundaries of the system and returns. The system does not exist in a vacuum and it may be influenced by the larger, exterior system, as when the culture provides a fatty diet, for example.

A cow may be seen as the focal point (the subset of closer relationships) of a system. She does not care what label we put on her but we can understand something of the nature of the creature by seeing her as a process of changing food into milk and manure. If the manure fertilizes her grass, we can note the feedback in the system. If her milk nourishes the farmer who feeds her during the winter, we can see both the feedback and the influence of the larger system within which the cow lives.

Individual people can be partially described as systems. Each of us processes stimuli and comes up with responses. Each of us does this differently, since we have unique ways of perceiving and being aware of stimuli and our own capacity for response. Poets are "turned on" differently than painters and they produce different results, whose influence comes back to them in different ways.

A family, a local community, a great university, a nation, or a number of allied nations may be understood partially in these terms. The "Spaceship Earth" is a system within our solar system. For all of these groups we see boundaries, a large environment that provides inputs, a focal point or points through which the exterior influences are processed and modified, some outputs, and the circular impact of the consequences as part of the next generation of influence.

In a political system we identify such stimuli as pressure group demands, underworld bribery and intimidation, political party nominations, campaign oratory and financing, and voter innocence and avarice. These are processed by government officials (lawmakers, executives, judges). The responses are visible as laws, executive orders, judicial verdicts, rewards, and burdens which in turn become grist for new efforts to influence the process. As part of the larger environment within which the political system operates, social work contributes to public policy at all three stages: input, processing, output. Social workers identify public problems and lobby for policies to alleviate them, they sit in the councils and administration of government, and they both shape and adapt to the responses.

A social work system

Mrs. Jones came to the walk-in Neighborhood Center because she was unhappy with her life. Her children had been sick a great deal this winter. Her husband had recently been laid off his construction job. Several bills were past due. The landlord was threatening eviction. Mrs. Jones herself was suffering from recurring headaches. As a last straw, her mother-in-law was planning to pay a prolonged visit. A neighbor had suggested the Neighborhood Center, and finally Mrs. Jones decided that she had to ask for help, though she had little idea what help she could expect.

Mrs. Jones liked the warm, friendly worker immediately. Gratefully, she accepted a chair and an invitation to "tell what is bothering you." As Mrs. Jones talked, she felt as if she were being heard. She felt that her troubles were important ones. But from the worker's comments, Mrs. Jones understood that she was not the only person to have them.

When she left, she had an appointment with a doctor at the outpatient clinic, and another with a family counselor. Even more important, she felt that she was doing something about her troubles. She had taken a first step.

The Neighborhood Center had certain functions which could be performed on the spot. Family counseling and referral to the Department of Welfare, the Department of Health, or Legal Aid, could be initiated there. To Mrs. Jones, the agency system was personalized by the worker who greeted her, asked what her problem was, and helped her answer the questions on a printed form. All the stimuli which had pushed Mrs. Jones to the agency were processed by the agency. They could not all be processed or even mentioned at once, but Mrs. Jones was able to feel that some start had been made toward alleviating some of her problems. Between her and the worker they were able to process some of the stimuli into some more satisfactory responses.

Mrs. Jones may be seen as a system; so may the worker. Both are parts of larger systems. Neither operates in a vacuum. Mrs. Jones and her family will affect the worker and the agency. The worker and the agency will affect Mrs. Jones and her family. The community in which they live affects them all. So does an even larger community. Some of the responses or output of Mrs. Jones's problems will be the result of her own efforts, some of the efforts of other people and institutions. The responses produce feedback which will have effects on Mrs. Jones' ability to manage other problems. If her headaches are cured, she may be better able to deal with her mother-in-law. If the family has legal advice, perhaps it can deal better with the landlord. In any case, Mrs. Jones will take in new inputs or stimuli and begin with the landlord.

A process of shifting relationships between parts of a larger whole can be noted in similar examples. The process is one of changing inputs into outputs. In each case the process takes place within boundaries. It is partly autonomous and self-generating because of the feedback, and partly the pawn of exterior forces.

System terms

We have already identified some terms—*input, output, processing, feedback*. Some other terms are also used frequently:

1. *Boundaries.* The boundary of a system may be physical—as in the skin of a person—or it may be less tangible—as in an individual's attitude toward sex—depending on the variables on which we focus. The boundaries of a personal system may include all of a person's roles, or only some roles, along with that person's biological system. The boundaries of a group may be the persons in the group, or the persons and their problems, depending on which variables we choose to focus on. The boundaries of a community or nation may be physical or philosophical. A nation-state may be bordered by two oceans; a community of scholars may be bounded only by the understanding of the participants in that community.

2. *Tension, stress, strain, and conflict.* Tension means the process of being stretched. Whatever is under tension is under stress and strain.

A combination of stresses and strains leads to conflict. Conflict is not necessarily good or bad, but when it occurs the system usually seeks relief. Television commercials are full of examples of individuals who are under tension, and who seek fast, fast relief. Political parties traditionally promise to give relief from whatever problems are producing tension at a given time. Relief from tension in a family system is a reason some people seek help from social workers.

3. *Equilibrium.* A system has a tendency to achieve a balance among the various forces operating upon and within it. Equilibrium refers to a balance, either still or moving. Equilibrium, like status quo, is desirable only for the people who realize some advantage from it. A welfare department system with a balanced budget may be maintaining equilibrium at the expense of hundreds of poorly maintained recipients. From the point of view of the latter, such equilibrium is not desirable.

4. *Intersystem.* An intersystem model involves two open systems connected to each other, and therefore interacting with each other. This interaction provides an extension of the systems theory, since it can be expanded to include the entire environment or condensed to include two very small systems.

5. *Connectives.* The ties of relationship between systems are called connectives. An example might be the contract or agreement between client and worker. It might be the worker himself, who is a connective between client and agency. Connectives may be dysjunctive, having a negative effect on the system's present functions. Which kind of connective would a social worker aspire to be?

6. *Developmental system.* A developmental system model centers around growth and directional change. The system under consideration —indivdual, group or organization—is growing, maturing, going somewhere. In this model, change is not random, or even planned, but growth-oriented. Phases and stages can be identified and predicted. This is a useful idea, but we cannot assume that future growth will reflect past growth, because there are too many other systems, too many variables to consider.

We have seen that there are several possible systems models. Each has peculiarities, but each has a common method of functioning. The components of a system that we identified follow each other in an orderly sequence: input, processing, output, feedback, and back to input.

For example, in a family, the father's new job is an input which disturbs the family equilibrium. The processing is done by the father but also by other family members who are affected by the new situation. (A change in part of the system affects other parts of the system.) The output may be increased job satisfaction on the part of the father and adjustment to a new neighborhood by the family. The feedback may be increased general self-confidence.

This process of changing something into something else is particularly important in the field of social work because it helps to identify and explain relationships between and within individuals, small groups and communities.

Individuals, small groups and communities
INDIVIDUALS

Social work has traditionally been concerned with individuals' behavior and their relationships with each other and with other aspects of their environment. Social workers have long tried to learn more about why people behave as they do. Early explanations included theories of human development, ideas about cause and effect, and assumptions concerning environment versus heredity.

Human devlopment. In this view of human behavior, individuals grow and develop at their own rate, but within broad limits. Children get teeth, and learn to walk and talk, in that order. The ages at which they do these things vary, but they must do them before they can go on to play running or singing games. A child whose development has been seriously interfered with at three months, six months, or twelve months, according to this view, will not be able to "catch up." One trouble with this theory is that it assumes a more positive knowledge of human development than we have. It seems presumptuous to assume that development of white, middle-class, U.S. children is a universal norm.

Cause and effect. Some of the same objections can be made to the theory that every cause has a single identifiable effect, or that every effect has a single identifiable cause. Early research in the social sciences indicated that many problems in society can be traced to many other problems. Thus, poor housing predicates juvenile delinquency, as do working mothers, broken homes, and many other "causes." One trouble with this is that sorting out causes and their resulting effects is often an overwhelming task. Another trouble is that, as in the human behavior example, we simply do not know enough to be sure we know all the causes and the effects.

Environment versus heredity. Like the two preceding approaches, the attempt to explain behavior in terms of environment versus heredity was an effort to simplify very complex social problems. At one time social scientists were willing to stake their reputations on one side or the other of this issue. The question of genetic and environmental influence could be argued, even though it was sometimes difficult to tell where one began and the other left off. A classic study of identical twins, separated at birth, served to satisfy the environmentalists, though the geneticists did not accept this proof. Terman's studies of gifted children as compared with a control group of average children indicated to the geneticists that high IQs predicated health, wealth and happiness. The environmentalists did not agree.

To say that all of these theories were bad and have been replaced by the systems approach would be an exaggeration. But the idea of a dynamic rather than a static approach has certain advantages. So does the idea of an approach which will apply to various sizes and kinds of systems, rather than to individuals only.

SMALL GROUPS

Michael Olmstead in *The Small Group* (1959) defines a small group as a plurality of individuals who are in contact with one another, who take one another into account, and who are aware of some significant commonality. For our purpose we will take a small group to include from two to about twelve people.

The small group is a system which may be separate and apart from the rest of a person's life. There are therapy groups, recreation groups, groups for a variety of purposes. The group system interacts with, but has a separate identity from and in addition to the sum of the individual systems which make it.

Figure 1 shows a group of hospital patients interacting with each other and with the hospital administration, and indicates some of the kinds of interdependence seen in group systems.

COMMUNITY

The community can be defined as either a geographical entity or as a functional entity. We refer to a city community or to a community of interest. Like the small group, the community involves individuals who are in contact with one another, but the assumption is that in the com-

FIGURE 1
Two diagrams of interdependence in group systems

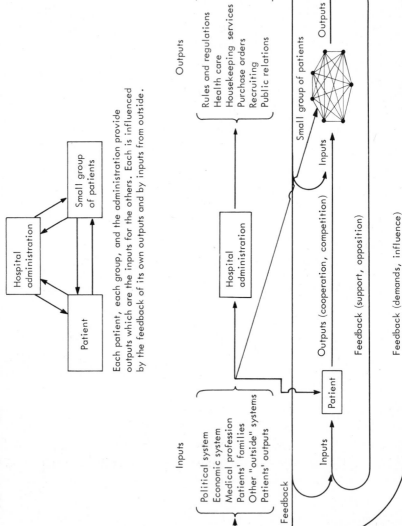

Each patient, each group, and the administration provide outputs which are the inputs for the others. Each is influenced by the feedback of its own outputs and by inputs from outside.

munity commonality is less significant and that the number of individuals is greater. It is possible to have a community made up of people who do not meet each other directly, as in the communities of musicians or scholars. The community is another system with which both individuals and small groups interact. The community is larger, more encompassing than the others, but this does not assume a greater or less degree of interaction.

In the Midtown Manhattan Study of Mental Health, described by Leo Srole and colleagues in *Mental Health in the Metropolis*,[1] the systems approach reflected the tremendous complexity of all the factors involved in the effort to find and explain incidences of mental illness.

Social work inputs: Planned change

So far we have talked about systems interaction and interdependence, and we have talked about change in terms of growth and direction in developmental systems. With some understanding of intersystems and developmental systems, we can look at another systems model, the planned change system. In this approach, it is not assumed that change in systems need wait on spontaneous, internal change or growth. In the planned change system, the change agent (for example, the social worker) intervenes at some point in the system. The intervention seeks to proceed in a predictable, orderly way.

If we take our earlier example of Mrs. Jones, we see that of all the systems affecting her at the time she approached the Neighborhood Center, the two most important at that time and in that place were her family and the social agency as represented by the worker. These were not necessarily the most important systems to her once she had left the agency or before she came, but at that particular time all else assumed less importance. In the same way, a community group seeking help from an agency is acutely aware of and responsive to the agency at the point of encounter, even though prior to the encounter the agency had been quite incidental in the community experience.

The same is true of a small group which meets for the first time in a juvenile court setting. Neither the group members nor the group leader are particularly interesting to individuals until the group becomes a

---

[1] Srole, Leo, et al., *Mental Health in the Metropolis: The Midtown Manhattan Study* (New York: McGraw-Hill, 1962).

reality. Then the setting, the agency and the leader assume overwhelming importance.

The steps in the planned change process used by many kinds of change agents, including social workers, follow.

1. *Perception of the need for change.* In Mrs. Jones's case, she became increasingly uncomfortable and unhappy with her life, but only at the suggestion of her neighbor did she decide to try to make an effort toward change. Being uncomfortable or dissatisfied or in pain may be the first step in perceiving the need for change, but the degree of discomfort which people find tolerable varies as much as do the people themselves.

2. *Initiating planned change.* The client may ask for help, as Mrs. Jones did. A teacher or school nurse concerned about the Jones children might have suggested strongly that she seek help. The social worker from the Center, hearing of the family's problems, might have called at the home to offer the services of the Center. Thus, the initiator might be the client, the change agent, or a third person.

3. *Establishment of a change relationship.* For social workers, this has traditionally been an important part of the change process. They believe that the character or quality of a relationship is important in all kinds of human interactions, but particularly in that between client and worker. This is true regardless of the time of interaction or of the size of the client system. A swift exchange of feeling is necessary to engender trust and engage the client system. This relationship is largely a result of input by the worker, whose attitudes, skills and knowledge will influence what the client thinks of him as a person and as a professional who is ready, willing, and able to give help. When the worker or a third person approaches the client, the worker needs even more skill at relating to the client because unasked-for "help" is hard to accept.

4. *Working toward change.* Here is the heart of the change process. Here is where many workers bog down. Once a need for change is felt, and the relationship is developed, what happens next? The client wants to know what the worker will do. The worker wants to know what the client will do. Some kind of mutual agreement constitutes a contract. If one step of the contract is filled, another step can follow.

5. *Generalization and stabilization of change.* The main test of the change agent's help is the stability and permanence of the changed behavior in the client system. Does the helping relationship promote

change which continues on through the rest of the client system, or is the change localized and limited? Change for its own sake is not a desirable goal. Unless the change process can be used again and again by the client system, the change agent has not been too helpful. There are great differences in susceptibility to change among various client systems. Also, the resources and skills of the worker or the change agent help to determine how well or how poorly change in one area can be continued in another.

6. *Achieving a terminal relationship.* Breaking off a relationship is an important part of the change process. The client system must be helped to know that its behavior has been fully successful only when it can part company from the change agent, but that this parting is desirable and necessary because it indicates that the modified client system is able to operate independently.

An enlarged and expanded explanation of the planned change process appears in Lippitt, Watson, and Wesley's *The Dynamics of Planned Change* (1958). The term *change agent* is used by those authors because their references are to many professions, including social work. As social worker-change agents, we take a number of roles. Some of these roles involve direct service to the client; some involve indirect or supporting service. A role is a set of expected behaviors—expected by the role player and by others. There are a number of possible ways to identify and describe social work roles. For our purpose, we will use the 12 roles outlined by McPheeters and Ryan in their monograph, *A Core of Competence for Baccalaureate Social Welfare* (1971).

Roles for social workers

1. *Outreach worker.* A social worker who identifies and detects individuals, groups, or communities who are having difficulty (in crises) or are in danger of becoming vulnerable (at risk) works as an outreach worker.

2. *Broker.* The social worker who steers people toward existing services that may be of service to them is called a broker in the same way that a stockbroker steers prospective buyers toward stocks which may be useful to them.

3. *Advocate.* A social worker who fights for the rights and dignity of people in need of help advocates their cause.

4. *Evaluator.*   A social worker who gathers information, assesses problems and makes decisions for action is, among other things, an evaluator.

5. *Mobilizer.*   A social worker who assembles, energizes and organizes existing groups or new groups takes the role of mobilizer. This is most often a community organization role, though not always.

6. *Teacher.*   A social worker whose main task is to convey and impart information and knowledge and to develop skills is a teacher. This role may or may not be played in a formal classroom situation.

7. *Behavior changer.*   A social worker who works to bring about change in behavior patterns, habits and perceptions of individuals or groups has the role of behavior changer.

8. *Consultant.*   A social worker who works with other workers or other agencies to help them increase their skills and solve clients' problems is a consultant.

9. *Community planner.*   A social worker who works with neighborhood planning groups, agencies, community agents or governments in the development of community programs is called a community planner.

10. *Data manager.*   A social worker who collects, classifies, and analyzes data generated within the welfare environment is a data manager. This role may be performed by a supervisor or administrator, or it may be carried out by a clerical person with the necessary skills.

11. *Administrator.*   A social worker who manages an agency, a facility, or a small unit is operating in the role of administrator.

12. *Care giver.*   A social worker who provides ongoing care—physical, custodial, financial—for whatever reason is acting in the role of care giver.

The important thing to remember about all the roles listed is that they are roles which combine with other roles. They are not jobs or positions. They are not necessarily related to the amount of education or training that a worker has. Most jobs in most agencies are made up of a blend of several roles. Example: A caseworker on a home visit talks with the neighbor of her client. The neighbor wants to know where she can get information on family planning. The caseworker gives the information and offers to make an appointment. Because she has had other requests, she makes a note of this, to support her feeling that the welfare department should publicize its service. Example: In a small rural agency, the supervisor allots cases, helps caseworkers with problems, supervises the clerical staff of one secretary, and prepares the office budget. Example: A caseworker visiting a new client learns of problems with the landlord. Because she recognizes the client's inability to complain, she volunteers to talk with the landlord herself. If this is not helpful, she puts the client in touch with the local rent control office.

These are examples of a caseworker who is an outreach worker, broker, data collector in the first instance; in the second, of a supervisor who is a data manager, administrator, evaluator; in the third, of a caseworker who is a broker-advocate. When we think of any job broken down into its roles, it is easier to see that the traditional skills (casework, groupwork, and community work) are complex and not discrete.

Summary

Social systems is a concept which social work has borrowed from the sciences to help explain and understand the relationships between ideas and things. Concepts of human development, cause and effect, and heredity and environment were earlier efforts to see relationships.

Any system is made up of subsystems enclosed by a boundary. Input from outside is taken in, processed, and put out, causing feedback. Because we know that this process goes on, we have also accepted the idea of planned change. Change may be haphazard or it can be consciously planned, worked out and terminated through a system's own efforts. These efforts may be supported and modified by a variety of change agents playing roles as broker, advocate, teacher, administrator, and so on.

3

Social work history

Much of the history of social work is to be found in the history of religion, in the history of world economics and trade, and certainly in the history of political states.

The preceding chapter showed something about the theory of interrelated systems and something about the interrelationships between the various methods of social work. Now we hope to show the relevance of other systems to the historical development of social work and how it has come to be a new system.

A system, we saw, is a phenomenon which can be broken down into subsystems or can combine with others to form a supersystem. Either way, the important concept is that of interrelationships, rather than of cause and effect. All parts of a system are affected by a change in one subsystem, and a change in the whole system changes all of the subsystems. Since we can never understand all of the systems which affect a given situation, we try to choose the most important interrelationships and draw conclusions from them. Inevitably, some changes can be effected consciously and rationally. Others may seem to be brought about by pure chance. But even changes that are brought about through chance affect the system and its parts.

Some systems affecting history

Traditionally, social work history is introduced by relating the giving of alms, according to Judaic-Christian ethic. Both religions, important in Western thought, urge charity through almsgiving, that

25

is, sharing with those less fortunate. Judaism goes back thousands of years before Christianity which itself is now nearly 2,000 years old. The degree to which the followers of either religion have followed its precepts is something less than complete. Some systems other than traditional religion must have an effect on social work. Economic factors must have some bearing. People who are affluent have more to share than those who have barely enough. For much of the world's history, the great majority of the people have had barely enough. Politically, the distribution of power has been linked with the distribution of wealth. Wealthy, powerful people have been in the minority but have made decisions for and about the majority. At least three systems, then, have affected the growth and development of social work: religion, economic, and political. Many other systems have also been involved; these are just the most outstanding examples of the interrelationships.

If religious influence were decisive, we might expect the rise of the Christian Church to have produced a tremendous system of charity during the first thousand years after Christ. This was not the case. As Christianity became widespread, the Church was intimately associated with the wealthy and powerful members of every community. Though the alms which were given were mainly the work of monks and monasteries, charity was not the all-out effort desired by the Church's founder.

In England, a number of laws were passed after the waning of the Middle Ages with the purpose of discouraging an increasing incidence of vagrancy. Vagrancy and begging increased as the stability of the villages decreased and as more people were attracted to the cities. The culmination of these laws was in the legislation best known to English and U.S. social workers as "43 Elizabeth" or the 1601 Poor Law. Passed late in the reign of Elizabeth I after a long period of relative peace and security, when England was more affluent and unified than ever before in its history, it called for each locality to be responsible for its poor and old and handicapped. It was a conscious effort at change in a system which had accepted and expected beggars from time immemorial. Confiscation of Church property during the reign of Elizabeth's father, Henry VIII, had deprived beggars of their usual source of maintenance. The government accepted some responsibility, and eventually, this responsibility was broadened to include employment, housing and health. But in 1601, *local* responsibility for the poor was a new idea. Elizabeth, herself a strong monarch interested in the welfare of her people, helped in the movement toward changing attitudes toward the indigent. The beginnings of trade and industry in a country not preoccupied by threats of war helped. So did the need for beggars as potential employees. Many other systems, both developmental and planned, converged to produce the laws now generally recognized as the beginnings of responsibility for the indigent. The major provisions of the law attempted to spell out a sense of responsibility.

1. Overseers of the poor were to be appointed annually by the justices in each parish. In addition to church wardens the overseers were to include two to four "substantial householders."

2. Able-bodied persons who had no means of support were to be set to work.

3. The funds necessary for implementing the act were to be raised by taxing every householder.

4. Power was given to the justices to raise funds from other parishes in the vicinity or even within the same county if insufficient funds were available locally.

5. Overseers were authorized to bind out poor children as apprentices, subject to the consent of two justices. A "woman childe" could be bound to the age of 21 or marriage and a "man childe" to the age of 24.

6. Local authorities, with the consent of the lords of the manors, were empowered to erect workhouses on waste lands. Building costs were to be borne by parishes or counties.

7. The mutual responsibilities of parents and children to support one another were extended to include grandparents.

8. Justices were authorized "to commit to the house of correction, or common gaol, such poor persons as shall not employ themselves to work, being appointed thereto by the overseers."[1]

These laws, crude and judgmental as they seem, were the basis for all legislation having to do with the poor in England and then in the United States for the next 300 years.

At about the same time, in 1617, St. Vincent DePaul founded the Ladies of Charity in France. His effort to foster a sense of responsibility for the poor among wealthy Frenchwomen was only partly successful, since the volunteers were not always dependable. In 1633 he founded the Sisters of Charity, who, once volunteered, were more reliable in visiting the poor, the sick, and the aged. But these were voluntary

---

[1] Crampton, Helen M. and Kaiser, Kenneth K., *Social Welfare: Institution and Process* (N.Y.: Random House, 1970), p. 7.

efforts in the name of religion. English poor law saw the state as responsible for the poor.

Refinements of the Poor Law included the Settlement Act of 1662 and the Workhouse Act of 1696. The Settlement Act required the return to their own parishes of any newcomers who might be judged to become dependent on the parish to which they had moved. Not until 1795 was the act amended to require that a person could be sent back to his home parish only after he had actually applied for relief. The Workhouse Act was an effort to require that paupers earn their keep through work contracted by private operators. In order to receive any relief, the laborers and their families had to live in the workhouses, separately, and under overcrowded and unsanitary conditions. Both the Settlement Act and Workhouse Act were designed to solve locally what were increasingly national and international social and economic problems. Both acts exemplified a philosophy which has continued well into the 20th century in this country as well as in England, namely, that personal responsibility for personal problems is the accepted norm, regardless of political, economic or social problems.

Not until the middle of the 19th century were the laws reformed, and again it was at a time of relative affluence on the part of large numbers of people. It was also a time of keen interest in and concern for law and justice, as well as of vague feelings of guilt at the presence of poverty in the midst of plenty. Industrially, England was producing more wealth than ever before in its history, but many people working with factory workers, child laborers, and the unemployed knew that the good effects of production were not filtering down to all the people. Economically and religiously, the country was ready for a new reform of the poor laws. Politically, too, people with power were willing to share, if not power, at least some of the material attributes of the power. However, this same moralistic strain produced a new idea of the "worthy poor" which was built into the reforms of 1834. The gist of the idea was that there were two types of poor people: the "worthy poor" were deserving of help and the "unworthy" were not. According to Kathleen Woodroofe, in *From Charity to Social Work,*

> It was believed that the public relief of destitution, financed out of taxation as distinct from the alms of the charitable, must have a demoralizing effect on the recipient. It sapped his initiative, degraded his character, and encouraged him to be thriftless and dependent. Moreover, by raising wages above the level of mere subsistence, such relief

encouraged the poor to multiply their numbers, and the wage increase was nullified.

Voluntary philanthropy, it was believed, was a far better solution to the very real problem of poverty. Helping the poor was a means of "assuaging that sense of personal guilt which lay at the base of so much of the humanitarianism of the Victorian period."[2]

Meantime, in the United States, a similar movement for reform was taking place. It came as something of a surprise to the rugged individualists of the New World to find that they too had a poverty contingent. Because population was sparse and resources plentiful, the first New World communities regarded poverty as an unusual and temporary situation. Almshouses for the containment of all who could not or would not be productive were the solution in the local community. However, the English philanthropic movement found its way across the Atlantic and a great variety of societies for the aid of certain groups were established.

As in England, the assumption that this would be a temporary situation, necessary only until the poverty group had been reclaimed and rehabilitated, gave volunteers and voluntary societies a kind of missionary zeal. But the New World had neither the experience nor the patience with nonproducers that England had. In the colonies and later in the states it was assumed that everyone who produced could share in the profits. This very simple economic theory was never true, and never took into account the old, the young and the handicapped. The theory also ignored the growing importance of slavery in the southern states. Though slaves were imported from Africa by all the colonies, they became an economic force in the South with the increasing importance of cotton production. Slaves were needed to plant, cultivate and harvest cotton, but their own efforts brought them little profit except through the good will of their owners. As an economic institution, slavery required that owners maintain their people in reasonable health, and presumably many slave owners took care of the old and the very young, as well as of those whose productivity was essential to production. Nevertheless, slaves who produced did not share immediately in the profits, but depended on the masters for their benefits. The system bred a paternalism at best, and exploitation at worst, and at least partly nulli-

---

[2] Woodroofe, Kathleen, *From Charity to Social Work* (London: Routledge & Kegan Paul, 1962), p. 17.

fied psychological and religious urging toward change in a system of organized charity in the South, long after northern organizations were operating.[3] Even when some southern communities set up some organizations, later in the 19th century, black clients were effectively excluded. The effects of slavery and all its economic, political and psychic subsystems continued to be present in the South through the 19th and well into the 20th century.

In the North and the West, almshouses were seen as the solution to nonproductive poverty. If people were able to produce, they could be at large; if not, they could be incarcerated. The main problem with this solution is that in spite of bad conditions in the almshouses, it was an expensive and unprofitable solution. It may have even offended the sensibilities of some of the religious members of the community. In any case, before long in the United States, as in England, voluntary societies for the relief of various categories of poor were initiated as the need was perceived by concerned people of the community.

During the mid-19th century in England several scientific studies of poverty were made, notably by Charles Booth, Beatrice Potter Webb and Edward Denison. They exposed something of the vastness of the problem of poverty in Britain. Booth's 17 volumes of *Life and Labour of the People of London,* carefully and painstakingly researched, convinced many Victorians that voluntary aids could not reach the numbers of needy. Nevertheless, the period saw the beginnings of the settlement movement. Education and encouragement in their neighborhoods, it was thought, could relieve the poor of the kinds of disadvantages most oppressive to them. One well-known settlement was started and continued by Samuel Barnett at Toynbee Hall in East London. His feeling was that the poor would benefit from the chance to "contact with those who possess the means of a higher life."[4] His colleague, Arnold Toynbee agreed with this view, and also saw that settlements were a means to social harmony rather than political socialism. The Victorians believed in the scientific method as a means of learning about the problems of the poor. They feared the possible power of the poor, but they responded with a faith in mitigation of conflict between classes, rather than in a change in the social order. Education and understanding were to work

---

[3] Fogel, Robert and Engerman, Stanley, *Time on the Cross,* 2 vols. (Boston: Little, Brown, 1974).

[4] Barnett, Henrietta, *Canon Barnett, His Life, Work and Friends* (London: John Murray, 1919), vol. 1, p. 307.

both ways. The wealthy would learn from the poor and the poor from the rich. Schools, both settlement-run and state-run, were patterned after industrial establishments, so that children would learn early the kinds of behavior which would be acceptable to adult employers. Group pressure was part of settlement house procedure, but most important was pressure from authority.

If settlement houses sound like a feeble reaction to the knowledge of poverty suddenly sprung on the Victorians, it must be remembered that the idea of any kind of social reform was new and radical in a very old country. Further, the new ideas were being put forth not by the traditionally wealthy and powerful aristocracy, but by clergymen, professors and businessmen. Settlements were a major breakthrough. In the United States, too, the settlement movement, though later in starting, affected the lives of the poor in big cities through the efforts of people like Jane Addams at Hull House in Chicago. In the United States, the tremendous immigration of the 19th century forced attention on the urban poor who were the main recipients of settlement work. Again the idea was to make the poor conform to prevailing norms, not to try to change the norms.

Nevertheless, reform was a part of the settlement movement. Education of poor people to their duties and responsibilities as citizens was stressed by Barnett and Addams. The neighborhood was seen as a subsystem of the state and the state as a subsystem of the nation. Thus, in the settlements, grassroots community work was practiced, though always within the framework of the existing organization.

The charity organization society

Amid the scarce public provisions for relief, the number and variety of voluntary organizations of the 19th century seemed overwhelming. An affluent class, troubled by their awareness of sin, and (according to Beatrice Webb) strongly influenced by a new awareness of scientific method, seemed determined to start a new agency for each new problem as it was perceived. Charles Loch worked from 1875 until his death in 1913 to bring about some order and organization to this profligate charity. Scientific method and a strong sense of duty seemed to him to give all people a chance to achieve self-dependence. Charity could only be useful if it gave the recipient a chance at this self-dependence. To this end, he organized a group dedicated to helping those who deserved help and turning away those who did not and, further, seeing that those undeserving should not receive help elsewhere. It was not an easy task, but a Charity Organization Society (C.O.S.) report from the time indicates the system used:

Class I: Dismissed as:

Not requiring relief	1,037
Ineligible	2,273
Undeserving	1,240
Giving false address	360
Class total	4,910

Class II: Referred to:

The poor law	1,413
District agencies	1,645
Private persons	1,157
Charitable institutions	469
Class total	4,684

Class III: Assisted by:

Grants	3,293
Loans	1,039
Employment	391
Letters to hospitals	425
Labour register	623
Class total	5,780
Grand total	15,374

This table, from the C.O.S. fourth annual report (1873), shows the care, organization and careful compilation of statistics which were the Society's contribution to voluntary charity. It also shows the kinds of judgments which were made by workers about the people who applied to them. Large numbers of undeserving supplicants did not meet the Society's formal requirements, which were designed to deter any who were not willing to help themselves.[5]

Even with these requirements, workers for the organization were expected to know and understand a great deal about their clientele. Thomas Chalmers, a Glasgow clergyman, emphasized the need for care in the selection and training of voluntary workers. He expected them to be of high moral ability and intelligence, and he outlined the kinds of questions they should ask, and the kinds of investigations they should

---

[5] Charity Organization Society, *Fourth Annual Report, 1873*, Table p. 2.

make. His contribution to social work was his emphasis on selection and training, as Charles Loch's was the initiation of the Charity Organization Society. Thus, we see that early social work in England was not purely casework but group work through the settlements, and community organization through settlements, the Charity Organization Society, and training and education through Chalmers' guides for voluntary visitors. In this group of pioneers, Octavia Hill's emphasis on casework premises of knowledge of the individual and on the one-to-one relationship was the forerunner of the psychological emphasis in today's casework.

State and local responsibility

The 19th century's preoccupation with local voluntary charities cannot be said to be the result of earlier centuries' poor laws. Neither can it be said to be caused by the century's affluence, industrial expansion, scientific knowledge or education. Rather, it was affected by all these rapidly changing systems to the end that no future period would ever again see the lack of activity in charity that prevailed in earlier times, both in England and in the United States.

In the United States, as the various states grew in power and influence, the initiation of state departments of charities and corrections or some similar organization became common. The purpose of these departments was implicitly and explicitly to save taxpayers money. Scarcity as an ideology was the accepted attitude. Whatever method of relief was given must be the least possible to maintain life. A means test and a pauper's oath were assumed to be not only desirable but necessary to make sure that no relief was given to anyone able to provide for himself. Outdoor relief, that is, relief given to people in their own homes, was considered to be more difficult to supervise and therefore more likely to corrupt.

> It is also generally known that those demanding outdoor relief are . . . members of the lowest [classes]. Regardless of all responsibility for it, they bring into the world a race of dependents, physically, morally and mentally deficient. But if, when these deficient and delinquent members of the lower classes give evidence that self support is impossible, they are retained in institutions properly regulated, while the individuals are cared for, propagation of their kind is at least checked.[6]

---

[6] *The Prevention of Pauperism*, Proceedings of the Sixth Annual Conference of Charities (Chicago, 1879), p. 214.

Institutions such as almshouses, hospitals and prisons were the chosen method of relief in most states. Only much later could the expense of institutional care be credited to state legislatures.

Still, U.S. citizens, like the English, felt uncomfortable with the idea of great poverty in a wealthy society. As in England, many U.S. citizens, including Charles Loring Brace, foresaw the dangers of gangs of boys adrift in large cities, preying on the unwary. Brace found his solution in organizing the Children's Aid Society of New York. The first organization of its kind, the Society undertook to remove children from the unhealthy slums of New York and send them to rural homes in the Midwest where, it was hoped, they would be treated as members of the family and learn to work along with the rest of the family. If the children sometimes took on the role of indentured servants, used by families only as a source of cheap labor, this was considered as aberration rather than a fault of the system. C. R. Henderson, in 1899 commented:

> . . . the homeless child is taken to a childless home, or to family care where love makes room for one more object of mercy and hope. . . . The old sad history is forgotten; with a new home begins new memories and a new career.[7]

Other kinds of voluntary organizations operated much as in England in response to perceived need. And, as in England, the Community Organization Society, first in Buffalo, tried to bring order from chaos through the same principles of investigation, registration, cooperation and friendly visiting as laid down by the London Society.

Gradually, through the end of the 19th century and into the 20th, the charity-giver and the radical joined forces, according to Jane Addams. From a firm conviction that poverty caused the delinquency of the individual came some recognition that the capitalistic system in a democratic framework produced more equality for the rich than for the poor. By the outbreak of the first World War, social workers and reformers had joined forces, at least in some matters, and social work had left the era of friendly visiting to become more professional and less apologetic about its function. Some people like Mary Richmond were beginning to press for training and education and even salaries for social workers.

---

[7] Proceedings of the 26th National Conference of Charities and Corrections (Cincinnati, 1899), pp. 12–13.

Mary Richmond

Mary Richmond happened into social work when she accepted the job of assistant treasurer to the Charity Organization Society of Baltimore at $50.00 a month. As she learned about the organization, she posited that charity is a great social force which should and could cooperate with workers of every variety of social belief. Her philosophy combined with an ability to administer and a genius for organization, and from assistant treasurer in Baltimore she moved to the position of General Secretary of the Philadelphia Society for Organizing Charity. Her favorite message was that of the necessity to combine casework with social reform.

When she became director of the Charity Organization Department of the Russell Sage Foundation in New York, she became involved in training and educating social workers, and it was then that she started work on her famous conceptualization of the social work process. She called it *Social Diagnosis* when it was published in 1917 and it is a classic today. For the first time, the social work process was described systematically in terms of fact-finding, diagnosis, planning and treatment. Though the emphasis is on the worker's activity, participation by the client is implicit. Her concern was with social casework and with a generic process by which all workers could proceed. Workers had been doing most of the kinds of tasks outlined by her for many years, but her clear, concise writing helped to pull the process together.

The work of Mary Richmond was another of the important influences on the development of the system of social work. Her writings came at a time when the current system was beginning to lose momentum. Richmond's emphasis on method did not ignore the need for values, sensitivity and a helpful relationship, but because the method was a specific new tool it was possible for workers to follow procedure implicitly, with little regard for the client's feelings. Richmond's intent had fewer followers than her method.

Freud and psychiatry

The effect of the writings of Sigmund Freud on the practice of social work, first in the United States and later in England, can hardly be overestimated. It seemed as if the system were looking for a change, a new direction, and the field of mental health provided the input. Custodial care for the mentally afflicted had been the rule until the late 19th century when Freud's work began to be published. Though Freud claimed success only for his work with neurotic patients, his theories of the dynamics of personality and of the unconscious focused interest on the causes of mental illness and the possibilities of treatment, rather than on custodial care. Clifford Beers' account of his institutional experience, *A Mind That Found Itself,* gave impetus to this interest. A committee organized for mental hygiene reported to the National Conference on Charities and Corrections in 1917 that the one science that had most to contribute, then or ultimately, to social work was unquestionably the science of the mind.[8]

The entry of the United States into the first World War brought new problems and new clients to social workers. They were, for the first time, dealing with people whose problems were not necessarily financial. Newly discovered psychoanalytic theories helped to explain and treat problems which seemed to originate in the individual's psyche. Caseworkers spoke of personal adjustment as the major purpose of their work, rather than personal independence.

Freud was not the only source of the new theories. Jung, Adler and Rank all contributed to the new emphasis on psychic problems and their solutions.

Differences between England and the United States

Important as theories were, they appealed more to U.S. than to English caseworkers. Different systems in each country produced different inputs, processing and output. The United States' traditional emphasis on individual difference, and "rugged individualism," bolstered by the Puritan ethic and an era of economic affluence all combined to distract social workers from social reform while they concentrated on individual adjustment. In England, social reform had gotten off to a better start. English social workers were more concerned with individualizing *services* to meet the needs of laborers, children and women,

---

[8] Copp, Owen, "Bearing of Psychology on Social Casework," Report for Committee Organized for Mental Hygiene, *Proceedings of the National Council of Social Work,* 44 (Pittsburgh, 1917), 104–12.

than with the personalities of the people. The idea of the welfare state was not anathema, but a reasonable goal to achieve the best life for the greatest number.

The United States had made some effort to organize voluntary contributions to voluntary agencies during and after World War I (this kind of activity appealed to the business community as a means of making social work more efficient), but not until well after the beginning of the Great Depression in 1929 was any formal national effort mounted toward public welfare. The Depression, with its accompanying unemployement and loss of private savings, provided a stimulus which local and federal governments could not ignore. At the beginning, the ideas of individual effort and expected recovery were employed by the federal administration under Herbert Hoover. Private welfare agencies were receiving less money and trying to do more work. State and local authorities were finding that their funds were grossly inadequate to deal with the number of applicants. Social workers found that personality analysis did not solve the problems of the jobless or the homeless. No one was feeling affluent. The Puritan ethic seemed to have gone astray, and powerful business interests were not powerful enough to re-elect a Republican administration. Roosevelt's New Deal was the first dramatic entry of United States government into the field of public welfare.

> The only thing we have to fear is fear itself. Our distress comes from no failure of substance. We are stricken by no plague of locusts. . . . Our greatest primary task is to put people to work. . . . I am prepared under my constitutional duty to recommend the measures that a stricken Nation in the midst of a stricken world may require.[9]

The first federal program to provide some relief for states' welfare efforts was the Federal Emergency Relief Administration (FERA), which at first provided some $500 million. Half of this amount was provided to states on a matching basis, half to states whose unemployment was so great or whose resources were so depleted that no matching funds were available. All FERA funds were to be administered through public agencies, and by professional social workers. While this program provided the first venture of the federal government into public welfare, its main objective was to provide unemployment relief for those persons

---

[9] Roosevelt, Franklin Delano, First Inaugural Address, March 4, 1933, in *Public Papers and Addresses*, vol. 2, pp. 11, 13, 15.

who had lost their jobs as a result of the Depression. Unemployables such as old people, children and the handicapped were not eligible. Work was considered a better solution than direct relief and many public works projects resulted. The term *emergency* indicated that the program was expected to be of short duration, and it was, partly because of criticism from various quarters. It was followed by the Works Progress Administration, the National Youth Administration and the Farm Security Administration. All of these provided more experience with federal-state-local cooperation, but none of them provided the kind of permanent organization for public welfare which was clearly needed. To this end, Roosevelt appointed a Committee on Economic Security made up of the secretaries of Labor, Treasury, and Agriculture, and the Attorney General and the Federal Emergency Relief Administrator. In January, 1935, the Economic Security Bill was submitted and, after many amendments, passed by the Congress.

The social security provisions finally became law on August 14, 1935, and because they had been watered down and categorized they fell far short of a welfare state. We can only surmise whether or not less attention to psychiatry and more to social reform might have produced earlier work on a better social security proposal, but the 1935 law hardly lived up to its title. It provided two proposals for social insurance, three proposals for general assistance, provisions for maternal and child welfare services, aid to the blind and to dependent and crippled children, and a plan to strengthen public health work. It provided nothing for the unemployed able-bodied worker whose plight had been the reason for government involvement in welfare. Its old-age pension proposal included a means test, and its social insurance provisions insured little. Nevertheless, the federal government was finally in the business of social welfare, and from 1935 to the entry of the United States into World War II in 1941, the country and the social work profession tried to sort out the workable aspects of the law.

In England, while the Depression also struck a bitter blow, some aspects of social welfare had already been taken over by the state. Workman's compensation, old-age pensions and compulsory contributory sickness and unemployment insurance had been in effect since before World War I. These and other public assistance programs had been occupying the English social worker's time and energy during the psychiatric era in the United States. England's post-war period was less prosperous than that of the United States, and its faith in the Puritan ethic had not persisted into the 20th century. England was generally better prepared to deal with economic disaster in the 30s and to move into a true welfare state after World War II.

With its usual traditional reluctance to move into "foreign entanglements," the United States became involved in World War II only after her allies had spent two years fighting. Fascism had been viewed with less alarm than communism. The United States had domestic problems which were overwhelming, and there was a general desire for peace and isolation. Nevertheless, the government's involvement in public welfare had paved the way for compliance with Allied aims even before the Japanese bombing of Pearl Harbor. Again, the social workers of the nation found themselves with clients whose needs were other than financial problems. The American Red Cross, the United Service Organizations and other voluntary agencies geared up again, and family service agencies pursued their Freudian way. Nevertheless, the Depression, followed by World War II, suggested to some social workers that national, even international planning might be the reasonable task of social work. Surely even the best-adjusted individual could not be expected to deal with such major catastrophes.

After World War II, social work in the United States played a larger part in all sorts of community organization, community development and community planning. Hesitantly at first, then with more assurance, the profession began to add to the theories and tasks which seemed to come within the purview of social work. At the same time, professional education became a more and more important preoccupation with social workers who had been practicing for most of their lives. The profession began to differentiate among its three main methods—casework, group work and community organization. The Council on Social Work Education attacked the task of identifying and describing the kinds of studies needed by all social workers for the practice of all kinds of social work. According to Werner Boehm in his article on social work education in the *Encyclopedia of Social Work*, in recent years schools of social work have usually accepted one of three forms for teaching social work methods:

> 1. The first model consists of schools' making available a concentration in a combination of methods, frequently casework and group work on the premise that there is similarity if not identity of principles between these two methods.
>
> 2. Other schools have made it possible for students to acquire a

generic base for the methods on the premise that there are some principles and concepts in each method that are not method-specific but
social work-specific and therefore need to be possessed by all social
workers who, in addition to their generalist function, also need a specific
method-determined function.

3. Still a third model operates on the premise that society currently
needs a social worker with skills in several methods of intervention.
Some schools thus seek to train a "generic" social worker whose knowledge and skill are undifferentiated as to method. These schools, in
fact or in theory, question the validity of the concept of method
differentiation.[10]

So important was social work education seen to be, that during the
50s and 60s many agencies, both public and private, were willing to
finance graduate studies for workers who were already practicing. Education generally, and social work education in particular, received tremendous support during those difficult decades—again influenced by
an era of economic affluence, the broadening power base in politics,
and a general faith in education to overcome the evils of urbanization,
industrialization, prejudice and bigotry. Social workers were in the
vanguard. Group workers, like caseworkers were carving out new em-
pires, trying new methods, and researching new theories.

At the same time, during the 60s, the nation, first under Kennedy
and then under Johnson, became involved in an effort to put an end to
poverty. Dramatic in its conception, the program followed a number of
earlier pilot programs aimed at improving the quality of life for
persons at the very bottom of the economic ladder. For the first time
poverty was to be attacked at its roots. The program was to involve a
new federal organization, was to work directly with communities
rather than through the states, and was pledged to involve maximum
feasible participation. The last requirement proved to be a bone of
contention, but also to be one of the lasting effects of the program.
Most of the projects, including Community Action Programs, Head
Start, Legal Aid and Vista, involved poor people. The plan was that the
poor should be actively involved in planning and staffing. For various
reasons, the federal administration preferred not to use existing welfare
departments, and regarded professional social workers as supporters of
the "establishment." While social workers resented this attitude, it

---

[10] Boehm, Werner, "Education for Social Work," *Encyclopedia of Social Work*,
1 (New York: National Association of Social Workers, 1971), 260.

forced them to reconsider their roles in working with the poor, and spurred more interest in the area of community work and efforts at changing the larger systems. Client participation in planning and programming was sometimes successful and sometimes not, but social workers learned that they could and should become involved with different systems in different ways.

With the 70s came economic recession, and conservative, authoritarian federal administration, along with a general distrust of education and educators. Social work turned its attention to programs for undergraduate students who could hope to practice in some of the positions formerly held by graduate workers, and both government and private agencies pulled out of the business of making grants for education.

In England the end of World War II brought a change of government and the advent of the welfare state. Heavy taxes on all citizens provided some degree of welfare for all. Social workers were busier than ever trying to meet the needs of children, pensioners and the mentally ill for housing, residential care and hospitalization. Social work practice through governmental authority took most of the energies of most social workers, though voluntary agencies still found needs not covered by the extensive state provisions. Social work education remained a rather small part of social workers' concern until the late 1960s when a plan for three grades of social worker went into effect.

Interestingly, community work was not seen as part of social work and group work had not made the same impact in England as in the United States. Most English social workers are caseworkers. They are trained for work in a particular setting, and expect to stay in that setting. With the 70s, fulfillment of this expectation seems unlikely. Social work education has become more prevalent, though there are still only a minority of universities or technical colleges offering education for social work.

If it is possible to compare social work in the United States with that in England, we might say that having sprung from a common base, they have gone in different directions. England, with its extensive system of public social services, has responded to inputs from socialistic ideology, broad governmental authority, and less self-searching. The United States, with its tradition of individual responsibility and self-determination, has produced social workers who have gone in their own directions, practicing a wide variety of social work and writing extensively about their experiments.

Summary

The history of social work has been closely tied to the history of religion, of economics, and of politics. Social responsibility has its roots in a pre-Christian era and has taken different forms at different times in history. Residual and institutional views of social problems have contributed to theories of social welfare and social work. The English poor laws and settlement laws provided models for public responsibility in the new world, and some of the basic premises of individual versus public guilt still have an effect today. The Victorians' respect for scientific method led to efforts at organizing and quantifying charity. Freud's studies of personality development led the way to individualizing social work. With the entrance of national governments into the welfare field, social work and social work education have become full-fledged professional fields both in the United States and in England.

4

Social casework

Social work is a process of intervention between two or more systems by one or more change agents. The process of intervening on an individual basis has been known, traditionally, as casework. Helen Harris Perlman says, in the first chapter of her book, *Social Casework: A Problem Solving Process:* "To attempt to define social casework takes courage or foolhardiness or perhaps a bit of both."[1]

However, Perlman, who is an authority in the field, goes on to suggest the following definition:

> Social Casework is a process used by certain human welfare agencies to help individuals to cope more effectively with their problems in social functioning. . . .
>
> The nucleus of the casework event is this: a person with a problem comes to a place where a professional representative helps him by a given process.[2]

Florence Hollis, another leading authority, says:

> Central to casework is the notion of "the person in his situation" as a three-fold configuration consisting of the person, the situation and the interaction between them.[3]

---

[1] Perlman, Helen Harris, *Social Casework: A Problem Solving Process* (Chicago and London: University of Chicago Press, 1967), p. 9.

[2] Ibid., p. 10.

[3] Hollis, Florence, *Casework: A Psychosocial Therapy* (New York: Random House, 1972), p. 10.

While experts in the field respect Perlman and Hollis as two different kinds of practitioners with differing outlooks, others can see remarkable agreement in their versions of the casework process. (Additionally, perhaps, we can appreciate the similarity between these two versions and the definitions of social work in chap. 1.)

These definitions indicate an awareness of the importance of the individual as part of various systems, outside himself. Perlman emphasizes the importance of *the agency* with all its subsystems and supersystems. Hollis indicates that the *situation* with all its ramifications is the concept to be dealt with.

Both agency and situation are important systems, not only in intervening with individuals, but with families, groups, and communities as well. There are some differences between casework, family therapy, group work, and community work, but there are also similarities. With all sizes of client systems, the planned change process is followed.

Initiating the planned change process

A variety of situations and initiatives may lead to social work intervention. The individual or group directly involved, the family, public officials, social work agencies, or others concerned may initiate intervention.

In the case of an individual, the perception of need for change may be a real discomfort, pain, or deprivation. A woman whose husband has abandoned her with no means of support for her small children does not have to wonder whether or not she really needs change. On the other hand, alcoholics or drug addicts may not feel any need to change their lives, though the need may be quite obvious to other people. Dissatisfaction with one's marriage, one's job, or one's housing may be enough to send some people looking for help, while others will not even think of doing so.

Another important consideration following the first step of perceiving a need for change is the individual's ability to ask for help. Even a strongly felt need may not lead to intervention if the person is inhibited about seeking assistance. Asking for help is a very difficult thing for many people. Most of us do not like to feel dependent on others for coping with problems that we think other people in our circumstances solve by themselves. Students frequently experience difficulty asking help from teachers; children dislike asking their parents for emotional help; old people dislike asking help from younger ones when it involves loss of independence and an admission of decreased competence.

Still, many requests for change come from the person most concerned, and some social workers have felt that this ability to ask for help is necessary before service can be rendered effectively.

The second possibility is that the felt need for change is transformed into action only through the action of some other party. Teachers, physicians, and judges are among the professional people who promote change initiation on behalf of others. Parents frequently initiate intervention on behalf of their children or other people's children. Friends, neighbors, and relatives may be the instigators of change on behalf of anyone they know.

The third possibility is that the initiator of change may be the change agent himself. More and more, it seems evident that the people most in need of help may have no intention of asking it, or may have no friends or relatives to instigate help. For these people the outreach role of social work is vital. Social agency branches are sometimes located in residential neighborhoods. Advertisements are placed in public transport or on television publicizing such services as abortion referrals and crisis counseling along with a telephone number. In one mental health center, social workers went out knocking on doors and introducing themselves in supermarkets, much as political candidates do, to make themselves known in the neighborhood. In such cases the social workers make the first contact and their potential clients respond rather than initiating the process of change. However the change is initiated, much of the rest of the process depends on the feelings engendered in the beginning and during the next step of establishing the change relationship.

The change relationship, as Biestek[4] suggests, is essential to the casework process. Indeed, it is essential to the entire social work process. While the establishment of the relationship seems a tremendous responsibility for the worker—and certainly it is—still there can be no professional progress without it. The worker is able to give it his attention, while the client, who is confused and upset by his need, may have little idea what to expect from the worker.

---

[4] Biestek, Felix P., *The Casework Relationship* (Chicago: Loyola University Press, 1957), p. 17.

If the worker can put himself in the client's place, even briefly, and try to imagine the appearance of the office, the receptionist, and especially the all-important worker, he may be able to get some idea of the client's feelings. Some students have gone to a clinic or a welfare agency to apply for assistance in order to glimpse what it might feel like to be on the other side of the desk. Perlman says, "the person who comes as a client to a social agency is always under a stress."[5] Particularly stressful is the situation which is interracial or intercultural. Because most agencies employ predominantly white, English-speaking workers, a client from a minority group may expect and, unfortunately, may encounter a worker who does not understand him or his problem, or who appears to lack this important understanding. Nevertheless, the worker who makes the effort, who feels sympathetic, who tries to put himself in the client's place has a good chance of relating to his client. It could be hoped that as workers recognize their own limitations and blind spots, they will work toward erasing them.

Important as the worker's feeling and involvement are, they cannot take the place of his knowledge and skill. The worker knows information and resources which the client does not, and the worker has skills in bringing the client together with this knowledge. To be most helpful to the client, the worker must not be carried away by his sympathy, but must be able to stand off and look at the client and his problem dispassionately. He must find a balance between involvement and distance.

The interview

As a result of some initiative, either by a prospective client or another concerned person, a contact between the change agent and the individual is established. The initial contact takes the form of an interview where the feeling of empathy we have been considering seems most important, even before the interview begins.

The word *interview* may be slightly overwhelming to a new worker who does not know how to proceed, but because he is trying to feel with his client, he makes an effort to be warm, interested, and at ease. And that is the first step in the interview. Since this is the first step in many social relationships, what is different about conducting an inter-

---

[5] Perlman, *Social Casework*, p. 25.

view? First of all, both client and worker know that they have met because the client has a problem he hopes the worker can help with. If the client does not understand this—if he is, for example, elderly, confused, or ill—then the worker's first efforts should be directed toward helping him to understand what he is there for. If the client knows why he is there, he should be encouraged to tell his story in his own words, as easily as possible. Sometimes, clients do not verbalize easily. They may need a great deal of help and must be asked many leading questions. On the other hand, some workers are more at ease asking questions and filling in forms than in listening to the client tell his story in his own way. Such a worker may interfere with the client's chance to explain his own position. Sometimes, the agency requires a certain amount of information, which the worker must get. In any case, a balance between initiative and restraint is important, and the worker's warmth and interest are vital so that his client will feel accepted as a part of the new system. Besides the client's verbal communication, the worker must be keenly aware of the nonverbal cues, such as nervous movements, trembling hands, blushing or pallor, shortness of breath, or a variety of other signs which are seen rather than heard. The worker should also be keenly aware of his own emotional signals. Does he find himself feeling particularly good about this client? For example:

When Ms. Adams came into the worker's rather small office, she was flushed, somewhat disheveled and bright-eyed. As the worker shook hands with her, she thought she detected the odor of alcohol on Ms. Adams' breath. Ms. Adams, the mother of three small children, wished to know if she were eligible for AFDC (Aid to Families of Dependent Children). As she described the difficulty she had had in making the effort to come to the agency, the worker decided that she was under considerable nervous strain, but that she was certainly not drunk.

Ms. Adams said, in a rush, that her husband had left home a week before, after a quarrel over money. She had thought the quarrel not particularly different from many others, and had not even felt upset when Mr. Adams did not come home that evening. She had money, and she felt sure he would return when "he got over being mad." Now he had been gone for a week and her money was gone. She confided in her friend and neighbor who was sympathetic, but who advised her to seek help. Ms. Adams had no idea where to turn for help. Her family and her husband's family lived 2,000 miles away. Desperately she searched the yellow pages of the telephone book and called a number for Family Service. She had been advised to come in this morning, but she had had to bring her children and she was concerned about their behavior in the waiting room. The worker responded to this immediate concern by asking if Ms. Adams would like to have them with her during the interview. Ms. Adams said she certainly would. When she returned with three little boys, aged three, four, and five, the worker produced a pack of cards and asked the boys if they would like to build a card house. Ms. Adams actually smiled, and was clearly relieved.

This brief account covers the first three stages of planned change. Which statements refer to the perception of need for change, to the initiation stage, and to the beginning of the relationship? Why were the children brought in?

Contract

If all goes well, before the first interview is over, both client and worker know what the problem is, and what alternative actions may be taken to alleviate it. This recognition by each of what he is expected to do, and what he can expect of the other, is known as a *contract*. This is a rather impressive-sounding word for what may be a very informal agreement. Sometimes, a contract may be only setting the time and place for another meeting. Sometimes, both worker and client agree on certain action which will be taken before their next meeting. In any case, the basis for the contract is that it involves mutual expectations. Both worker and client are responsible for doing something.

William Schwartz, whose writing deals mainly with groups, but whose concept of contract is applicable to all of social work, lists five central social work tasks.

> 1. The task of searching out the common ground between the client's perception of his own need and the aspects of social demand with which he is faced. [The worker tries to find out exactly what the client sees as his problem, and whether this seems to fit with what seems to be the reality of his situation. "Common ground" is a reconciliation between what is and what the client would like.]
> 2. The task of detecting and challenging the obstacles which obscure the common ground and frustrate the efforts of people to identify their own self-interest with that of their "significant others." [Obstacles

may be real or imagined, but the worker's task is to decide which is which. Once identified, the obstacles may be challenged or dealt with by worker and client together, so that the client will not see himself as alienated from other people who are important to him, that is, his "significant others."]

3. The task of contributing data—ideas, facts, and value concepts— which are not available to the client and which may prove useful to him in attempting to cope with that part of social reality which is involved in the problems on which he is working. [The worker probably knows about community resources which he can suggest. His own agency may offer some services which the client can use. More than that, the worker's knowledge of human behavior, social policy, or his own human values may be new to the client.]

4. The task of "lending a vision" to the client, in which the worker both reveals himself as one whose own hopes and aspirations are strongly invested in the interaction between people and society and projects a deep feeling for that which represents individual well-being and the social good. [The worker is not currently under stress, and he has a background of success in dealing with people and their problems. He can share his experience and his values with the client, putting himself into the relationship, showing his concern and hope for a successful resolution.]

5. The task of defining the requirements and the limits of the situation in which the client-worker system is set. These rules and boundaries establish the context for the "working contract" which binds the client and the agency to each other and which both client and worker assume as their respective functions.[6] [Having shown the client that the worker is interested, that the agency offers services, and offered some hope for resolution of the problem, the worker sets the stage and provides the rules which both the client and worker will follow. It is important to note that the emergence of a contract is part of the change process, but that the development of a relationship precedes any effort to establish the contract.]

The caseworker, striving to put these central tasks into practice, will listen carefully and sympathetically to the client's version of the problem as he sees it. The worker will then try to describe what the agency can or cannot do, and more specifically what he personally can and cannot do. The client should have an opportunity to accept or discard these proposals. If client and agency perceive some common ground between client need and agency services, then they have a contract. For example:

---

[6] Schwartz, William, "The Social Worker in the Group," *Social Welfare Forum* (1961), p. 157.

Knowing that her children were taken care of, Ms. Adams proceeded to relate a story of marital problems, employment, and housing, and money problems. She had no idea where her husband had gone and no idea what she could do until he returned. She hoped the worker could help. The worker outlined the agency purposes and policies, the arrangement for temporary aid, and the necessity for making an effort to find Mr. Adams. At first, Ms. Adams protested that she did not want to find him. If he did not care about her and the children, she did not want him to return. But how, the worker asked, could she support herself and her children? Ms. Adams did not know, but she felt sure that her husband would return, would be sorry for what he had done, and everything would be all right. The worker said she hoped that this would be the case, but explained again, that in the meantime, some effort would have to be made to find Mr. Adams. Ms. Adams asked angrily if the worker would like to have *her* husband checked on by the police. The worker replied that she knew it was hard to consider this possibility, but that this was one of the requirements for getting aid from this agency.

Which of Schwartz's central tasks are exemplified in the foregoing? Did the worker respond appropriately to Ms. Adams' anger? Should the worker have explained the reason for the search policy? How else could Ms. Adams' objections have been handled?

Lawrence Shulman, in describing the contract, says:

> This contract will serve as a guide for the work they will do together. It has been openly arrived at and may be openly changed. While it stands, however, it serves to clarify the nature of the group's work and protect this work from "subversion" by group members, the worker or the agency.[7]

If we substitute the word "client" for "group" and "group members," we have a good picture of what goes on in this step of the casework process.

The work referred to by Shulman is the real heart of the casework process. Here alternative plans are developed, considered, discarded, or accepted. Important in this stage is the worker's recognition of the client as an individual with a right to work out his own destiny, to manage his own life. Because a client has decided, or been forced, to

---

[7] Shulman, Lawrence, *A Casebook of Social Work with Groups: The Mediating Model* (New York: Council on Social Work Education, 1968), p. 67.

ask for help does not mean that he is unable or unwilling to participate in his own plan. It is tempting to tell people what to do when they ask for advice, particularly when the solution seems obvious. But advice is rarely taken, and if it is taken, the outcome is rarely successful. Clients are more likely to make a success of their own plans than of an expert's. Social workers have worked hard and long to get rid of their images as givers of advice, as people who tell others what to do, and continue to do so.

In making a contract, the worker and client are really working together in an interdependent and symbiotic way. Each needs the other to carry out his part of the contract. On mutual understanding and respect will depend the next stage of the planned change process. Generalization and stabilization of change is the main test of the change agent's or worker's help. If the work jointly decided on tried out in a specific situation can be carried out in other situations and in other settings, the change can be said to be generalized and stabilized. If, on the other hand, the client is trying to please the worker, or to do what he thinks the worker wants him to do, then the change is probably not stabilized or generalized. The worker who tries to do everything *for* the client instead of *with* him, has made impossible the generalization of change, because the client will be unable to do for himself what the worker has done for him. Questions to be asked about the generalization and stabilization of change are: Can the client feel a sense of satisfaction and achievement, as a result of the efforts? Can he point to feelings before and after with pleasure? For example:

Ms. Adams said she certainly had to have money—and soon. How soon could she get some? The worker suggested that together they look at the most pressing needs, and try to figure out an emergency budget. Ms. Adams said she must have bread and milk and eggs for the boys. The worker agreed that these were necessities, and congratulated Ms. Adams on seeing the important things first. Ms. Adams knew nothing about her husband's finances, and had no idea if he had a checking account. In any case, she had never written a check. She reminisced about her life before she was married. She had worked in a mail-order house, received an envelope containing cash each week, and had no one to report to as to how she spent the money. The worker said that must seem very good to her now. But in the meantime, how far would $20.00 go toward groceries for a week? Ms. Adams knew exactly what she paid for various items and agreed that that sum would certainly

help. The worker asked her to bring receipts and the boys' birth cer-
tificates next week. By that time, the application would be underway.
When Ms. Adams told the boys to pick up the cards, they did so with
only a little complaint. The worker told them that they had been very
nice guests, and invited them back next week. Ms. Adams smiled and
thanked the worker. She said she did not like the idea of searching for
her husband but she guessed it was necessary. The worker gave her an
appointment card for the same time next week.

What was the work being done in this exchange? How was interdependence shown? Should the worker have let Ms. Adams talk more
about her early life? If so, why? What systems other than the family
are referred to in this passage? How do they affect Ms. Adams? Even
in this first interview, can you see instances of contract and stabilization
of behavior?

Finally, the last step of the change process must come. With some
resolution of the problem, some achievement of a goal, the relationship
must terminate. To the surprise of many clients and many workers, this
is often a painful step. If it was difficult to begin a relationship, it is
also difficult to end one. Again the worker may have strong feelings
about himself and the client, but he must remember that the client has a
bigger stake, has taken more risks, and feels more dependence. Therefore, it behooves the worker to help the client to terminate, despite the
worker's own feelings. He must recognize and accept his own feelings
of separation, at the same time that he recognizes the client's difficulty
in accepting the end. The client may be resentful, hostile, or deliberately
uncaring. Like any separation, this one will cause fears and doubts,
and perhaps regression to earlier behavior. Because the worker has
tried to develop the relationship, he may feel guilty about breaking it
off. The client may well perceive this guilt and try to make the most of
it. If anything, the worker is expected to be more accepting and understanding in this stage than in any preceding stage. He must also be firm
about setting limits. For example:

Ms. Adams returned for her appointment the next week without
the children. She would not need any more assistance. Mr. Adams had
returned on Sunday, and she would have no more financial problems.
The worker said she was very glad to hear that. Would Ms. Adams be
interested in marital counseling? Ms. Adams said, in an annoyed tone,
that this would not be necessary. She was certainly glad that she had
not let the agency search for her husband. The worker said that she was

glad it had not been necessary, but reminded Ms. Adams that the agency was available if the need should arise.

If you were the worker would you have offered counseling? If so, why? Why do you think Ms. Adams refused the offer? What feelings are shown by Ms. Adams? What feelings are shown by the worker? Do you think this was a satisfactory termination?

Termination was achieved, in the sketch above, because of intervention by outside conditions. Termination, like initiation, can also be achieved through conscious planning by either the worker or the client. Ms. Adams might have chosen to discontinue the relationship for a number of reasons which seemed valid to her. She might or might not have decided to let the worker know of this decision. The worker might have been able to arrange for Ms. Adams to receive AFDC, and then to transfer the family to a payments worker, with the worker and Ms. Adams mutually arranging this kind of termination. If clients do not always include workers in their plans for termination, workers must recognize their responsibility to include clients. Since social workers are trained to work *with* their clients, rather than *for* them, they will see the termination as a logical step in the planned change process, a contract which the client understands and accepts.

Sometimes before the foreseeable end of the planned change process, unexpected termination must come about, because the worker or client or both leave the area. If the worker leaves the agency, or at least the unit which serves the client, it is important to explain the reasons to the client and to mutually explore the necessary activities to effect a transfer. Perhaps a conference with the new worker can be arranged before the old worker leaves. At least the client must be appraised of the plan and given a chance to communicate his feelings. If the client is the one to leave, the worker should indicate the agency's concern by offering to refer the client to another agency, if possible. Sometimes that is not possible, but by the offer the client may be made to feel that he is worth some attention even though he will no longer be around. Perhaps he will want to call the worker, or write. Without fostering a sense of dependency, the worker needs to convey his sense of concern. Sometimes, clients simply leave without giving the worker a chance to react. Then the worker must deal with his own feelings. It is hard not to feel that the worker is at fault, and perhaps more thorough evaluation will reveal some problems which can be avoided in the future.

Any discussion of termination can hardly ignore the need for evaluation. Evaluation of the planned change process must certainly continue on the part of both client and worker all through the effort, to make sure that the original assessment still seems valid, and that they are proceeding along the right track. According to Pincus and Minihan, there are at least two major reasons why the social worker reviews and evaluates the change effort.

> The first has to do with his professional obligation to the client and action system members to indicate to what extent the outcome goals agreed upon in his contract with them have been realized. The credibility of the profession of social work rests on its ability to demonstrate that it can bring about the changes it claims to be able to make. Though this is usually considered to be a research problem, it is not just that. Generalizations about social work intervention must be based on a large number of cases, but it is still necessary to measure change in individual planned change efforts. The better the practitioner does in demonstrating and documenting the results of his work in each case the easier it will be to conduct needed research. Thus the first reason for evaluation and review stems from the fact that the worker is accountable for the results of his planned change effort to the specific client as well as to the general public which supports the profession.
>
> A second reason for the evaluation is that an explicit review and assessment of failures and accomplishments can be a valuable learning experience for those involved in the planned change effort, including the worker. It can help consolidate the lessons learned as a result of going through the planned change effort and can enhance the ability of the client or action system to cope with similar situations in the future. Thus even if mistakes were made and not all the outcome goals were realized, if those involved learned why the goals were not accomplished and how to avoid similar mistakes in the future, the planned change effort will have some payoff.[8]

Other systems

So far, most of the discussion of the casework process has emphasized the change in the client himself. In an earlier era, this might have been accepted as the the total purpose of casework. Now we recognize that some problems are not within the individual, but must be dealt with through other systems. To expect people to adjust to every other system is clearly unrealistic.

William Schwartz, the group worker whom we cited earlier, views

---

[8] Pincus, Allen and Minihan, Anne, *Social Work Practice* (Itasca, Ill.: F. E. Peacock Publishers, 1973), pp. 273–74.

the worker in the role of mediator between systems. He sees all systems as mutually interdependent, and therefore sees problems as situations which need mediation between systems.

Clients whose complaints involve other people, institutions or organizations may have just cause for complaint. Perhaps the landlord *is* making unfair profit on a hapless tenant. Perhaps the teacher *does* have it in for the complaining child. Perhaps the judge *did* impose an unjust sentence. Certainly when we look at the variety and complexity of intersystems relationships, we can hardly assume that our client is always the one who needs to be changed. In fact, when we look at the variety and complexity of intersystems relationships we may be likely to think that everything needs changing except the client. What can be done to help a child from a broken, deprived home? If he is a black youngster in trouble with school, police, and juvenile authorities, it is hard to believe that the fault lies with him entirely. Poverty, poor housing, lack of a role model, institutional racism, lack of motivation, and earlier inadequacies in his background can all be blamed on other systems. The trouble is that the other systems are frequently inaccessible to change. Perhaps the young man has already been sentenced to punishment or committed to treatment. The worker still has the responsibility to listen and encourage, to try to form a warm relationship. From there, his performance of Schwartz's five central tasks becomes crucial in helping the youngster. The first three tasks—searching out common ground, detecting and challenging the obstacles which obscure the common ground, and contributing data, facts, ideas and value concepts which are not available to the client—all these are real contributions by the worker to a young client who admittedly has many points against him. In addition to sympathy and support, the worker is dealing with the very real problems in a realistic way. The fourth task, that of "lending a vision" to a client, provides a very special dimension to the relationship. The worker whose life experience may or may not be better, but is certainly different from that of the client, can share with the client his own feeling of individual worth and social good. Finally, he can set limits and requirements so that the client will know that in this relationship, at least, he can expect consistency. The purpose of all this is to give the client a firm sense of his own self-determination, even in a limited way. He will be helped to feel that even though life has not treated him fairly, still he can do something about it, and that he can depend on the worker to help him do something about it.

For most workers, however, reliance on the client's ability to adjust to or make the best of a bad situation, will not suffice. Most workers will want to do something to change the systems which contribute to the bad situation. While the worker cannot change everything, he can accept his responsibility to mediate between his client and some parts of the system. He probably cannot change the judge's sentence, but he may be able to talk with the court counselor about this particular judge. Does he have some biases which may yield? Is he up for re-election? Is there a movement for reform of the juvenile court system? These are increasingly longer-range goals which may not help this particular client. But workers realize that their efforts on behalf of the client reach far beyond the interview, even beyond the personal relationship. On the other hand, the mediating worker may find that the young man's school is amenable to the suggestion that he receive special tutoring, or even that he change classroom instructors. Maybe bringing the family into the picture—or getting some of them out of it—will help everyone concerned. The point to remember is that many systems are affecting and affected by this individual. Intervention in some systems may help a great deal to straighten out others. Neither worker nor client can effect complete change, but change on a small scale may spread to other systems.

Change models in casework

So far we have looked at the steps in the change process and at the systems which may need change, or be available for change. Now we need to look very briefly at some of the philosophical bases for bringing about change. As we do this, we must remember that all of the theories and techniques mentioned are eagerly espoused by some worker, particularly by their authors.

Early casework was nearly always a matter of providing urgently needed goods such as food, clothing, a job, or rent money. It is fascinating to read early accounts of the interviews between worker and client. Home visits were the rule, rather than the exception, and workers seem remarkably unself-conscious about giving advice freely and frequently.

As casework became a more sophisticated process, two separate schools of practice emerged. One was called the *diagnostic school* and leaned heavily on stages of human development as explained by Freud. The second was called the *functional school* and emphasized the importance of human and agency functions and their interrelationships. While these differences seem in retrospect to be minor, compared with the amount of personal involvement and skill which every worker uses, still they were important in their time, and whole schools of social work were founded based on these differing philosophies.

The diagnostic-psychoanalytic school took its cue from the ego psychology writings of Sigmund Freud and later of Erik Erikson, who theorized that every human being goes through certain stages of growth, each of which is vital to his overall development. Certain stages are more likely to prove stressful than others, and the lack of resolution of one or more of these stages will prove permanently detrimental. Through long, involved casework, the client may be able to gain insight into the root of his difficulty and may eventually be able to understand his need for defenses. Once he understands, perhaps he will recognize that the defenses are no longer necessary, and will abandon them. For example:

Ms. Riggs was referred to the medical social worker by her doctor after extensive tests showed no physical basis for her persistent shortness of breath. The worker showed her concern and interest in Ms. Riggs, rather than in her symptoms. She took a rather exhaustive social and family history, that is, she asked Ms. Riggs to tell her about her childhood, her relationships with parents and siblings, about discipline, particularly as it related to toilet training and sex play. She learned that Ms. Riggs had been afraid of her father, particularly after she started to date. He had been very strict about her boyfriends and the hours she kept. Marriage had been a way out, and at first she had been very happy. But Mr. Riggs demanded sexual relations "all the time," and Ms. Riggs found that she was becoming short of breath when he was due home from work. The worker asked if she had ever felt that way before. Ms. Riggs said, with some surprise, that she had felt the same symptoms when her father was waiting for her after a date.

While this is an oversimplification, it does give some picture of what a diagnostic caseworker would do. This model contains many of the basic qualifications of social work, such as acceptance, recognition of individual dignity, and self-determination. Children's relationships with their family are certainly important in determining the kind of adult they will be. But the relationships are interdependent, and ongoing. As children are affected by their parents, so do they affect them. Older brothers and sisters are jealous of younger ones, but so are younger ones jealous of older ones. Furthermore, as people grow, they change, not just through childhood and adolescence, but presumably throughout life till death. Diagnostic thinking must take all systems into account.

A worker of the functional school, on the other hand, would see the client and his problem in relation to his agency and its functions. He would see the client as an independent individual, able to use or discard services offered by the agency. For example:

Mr. Brooks came to the family agency on the advice of his mother-in-law. He and his wife had been having very serious quarrels, and he was afraid she would leave him. The worker was sympathetic and hoped the agency could help. But she wanted Mr. Brooks to understand that it would be necessary to bring his wife, at least to some meetings. Also, appointments would be made once a week for six weeks. After that, both Mr. Brooks and the worker would decide if more time was necessary. Since the agency did not allow home visits, Mr. Brooks would be responsible for getting to the office on time for appointments. In some ways, the functionalists were closer to current schools of reality therapy and behavior modification than to the diagnostic school. Functionalists dealt with the here and now, rather than with the there and then.

Perlman and Hollis are both members of the diagnostic school, and their writings are highly recommended for students interested in pursuing that method. Both writers have become less puristic in recent editions of their basic texts: *Social Casework: A Problem Solving Process* by Perlman and *Casework: A Psychosocial Therapy* by Hollis. In any event, the dichotomy between the two schools is more interesting historically than currently.

Reality therapy was introduced by William Glasser, a psychiatrist, who was trained in the psychoanalytic method. His book, *Reality Therapy* (1965), describes his interest in making the client or patient more responsible for his own behavior. It rejects the classic concept of mental illness, which supposes that people are not responsible. It considers the conscious mind the only area which can be reached by therapy. But not only must the individual be conscious, he must also feel that he or she is worthwhile and lovable, that someone cares. This is the basis for reality therapy. The client is living right now in a certain situation which he can affect. The involvement of the worker or therapist is an important aspect. The worker is not removed or objective, but very much concerned with the client. The worker cares, and lets the client know that he or she cares—but *not* interested in excuses or explanations. The worker realizes that the client has had tremendous problems to overcome, but the worker has confidence in the client's ability to overcome them. This method leans heavily on self-determination and assumes a great deal of client responsibility. Glasser, who is the leading proponent—claims to have great success with all kinds of clients. Here is an example of reality therapy.

Kevin arrived for his first appointment with the court counselor. Sulky, but handsome, Kevin said defiantly, that he was tired of always being the fall guy. His arrest had been a frame, the cops had it in for him. The counselor responded sympathetically, but firmly. Kevin might not like having to report, might not like his job, might not like probation at all. Nevertheless, the court's rule was definite. Kevin was in trouble and what could he do to get out of it? Kevin insisted that it wasn't his fault. The other guys were the troublemakers. He had been the one to get caught. Still sympathetically, the counselor replied that neither he nor Kevin could change the court's ruling, but between them they might be able to give Kevin an easier time the next six months. He emphasized that he was vitally concerned in Kevin's successful probation, but said Kevin would be the one to make it successful or unsuccessful. When Kevin fantasized about what he would like to do to the cops, the counselor interrupted, directing Kevin to talk about what he could really do on a job. When Kevin suggested that he might work as a bag boy, the counselor encouraged him to mention possible employers. He suggested that Kevin see the employers on his list before next week and be prepared to report on his job-seeking efforts.

Reality therapy uses many of the casework principles which are applicable to all of social work, and Glasser has been very successful with groups, who support and criticize each other, in the same way that the therapist supports and criticizes. Reality therapy is a functional approach.

Behavior modification is a model developed by clinical psychologists. Original work was done by Pavlov, whose dog was presented with food and a ringing bell simultaneously. The food evoked a salivation response. The bell did not. After many repetitions, the dog linked the bell to the food and produced salivation even without the food. This type of conditioning is called *respondent* or *classical,* and depends on the subject's own behavior producing the feedback.

Further work which has been more important to social workers has been pioneered by B. F. Skinner and is called operant conditioning. Skinner theorized that behavior is controlled by its consequences. If the behavior is rewarded, it will appear more frequently. If it is not reinforced, it will appear less frequently.

> In behavior modification, the main focus is on observable responses, rather than psychic causes. . . . Most behaviorists allege that symptoms are no different from other responses, in that behavior (1) falls predominantly into the respondent or the operant realm, (2) was learned through processes of conditioning, (3) obeys the same laws of learning and conditioning as does so-called normal behavior, and (4) is amenable to change through the careful application of what is known about learning and behavioral modification.[9]

The behaviorist seeks to learn what specific behaviors the client sees as a problem. How often do the behaviors occur? What is the stimulus which elicits the behavior? To determine the answers to these questions, the worker may observe the client in a natural setting, or may accept the client's self-report, or may use some experimental technique to stimulate the natural stimulus-response.

Once the assessment is made, with the client's full participation, techniques for modifying the behavior may be decided upon. Operant conditioning includes positive reinforcement, extinction, differential reinforcement, and response shaping. Behavior modification practitioners are less interested in the reason for behavior than they are in changing it. They are skeptical of the use of insight, and they think that behavior, not intent, is the basis for the well-being of individuals, families, or groups. Some practitioners give rewards for good behavior, while others punish bad behavior. The main thing is that the rewards or punishments be consistently given, so that the subject knows the connection between the behavior and the reward or punishment.

Proponents of this method are enthusiastic about its merits in dealing with clients with varying kinds and degrees of incapacity. They point out its use in working with the mentally retarded, the mentally disturbed, normal school children, and mature adults. Furthermore, training workers in this method is relatively simple, so that ward aides, teachers, and prison guards can use the system of rewards or punish-

---

[9] Thomas, Edwin J., "Social Casework and Social Group Work: The Behavioral Approach," *The Encyclopedia of Social Work*, 2 (New York: National Association of Social Workers, 1971), 1226–27.

ment. Its success does not depend on verbal skills of the patient. Finally, they say, it works. For example:

Judy was a mildly retarded nine-year-old who attended a special class in a large public school. Her behavior prevented her and the other children from concentrating on the work at hand. The teacher initiated the token system, giving each child a token for a finished assignment. At first, Judy received no tokens, while some of the others received three a day. The other children redeemed their tokens for candy at the end of the day. The next day Judy got a token. She was so proud of it that she was reluctant to redeem it.

Those who oppose behavior modification suggest that clients are deprived of their right to self determination. The treatment takes away their human dignity. The film, *Clockwork Orange* is a science-fiction example of the kind of abuses which might occur under the use of behavior modification. Abuses can occur whenever people intervene in other people's lives, and a model cannot be defended or denounced on the basis of possible abuse. Like other models, behavior modification has value in helping people with their problems. Like other models it is not a panacea for all kinds of problems.

Summary

Social casework is one kind of intervention used by social workers. It employs the planned change process, and deals mainly with individuals in a one-to-one relationship. The interview is the usual method of communication, and the establishment of a relationship is followed by the making of a contract. The worker and client work together toward the solution of the problem and, eventually, the relationship is terminated by mutual consent.

Some of the more recent methods of intervention are based on the earlier efforts of social workers to practice different philosophies. Reality therapy and behavior modification are examples of methods which can be used with individuals, families, groups and communities.

5

Social work with families

Social work with individuals is known as casework, and usually involves a worker and one client. But as we saw in chapter 4, individuals can rarely be considered by themselves. For most people, the system with which they are most closely related is the family. Caseworkers have always known this, and nearly all caseworkers take the family into account, either personally or indirectly, when they work with an individual.

What is a family? Basically, it is a small, primary, face-to-face group. The members may be related by blood or by marriage, or, we must now recognize, may not have any formal relationship. Traditionally, its functions have been to develop its members, socially, physically and emotionally. Even in informal, unrelated groups, these functions are viewed as necessary and desirable and are carried on to some extent. The family system is, therefore, a link between the individual system and the larger society and, as such, it merits attention from anyone who is interested in social services.

Just as some individuals are better able than others to cope with life's problems and tasks, so are some families better able to cope. First of all, members of the family must be able to function as individuals, and then in their roles as members of the family. Secondly, they must be able to cope, both as individuals and as family members, with the demands made by larger systems. For example, a man must have a feeling of his own worth, but this is related to his worth as a husband, a father, an employee and a wage-earner. If there were one prescribed measure of performance, this would be difficult enough, but the rules keep changing. Men who were brought up to be hardworking and thrifty, to support their families and "get ahead," may find that society—or their own children—do not accord them the honor and respect which they feel is their due. Other men, because of race, lack of education, lack of motivation, or some other reason, may be unable or unready to work steadily and be good providers. As they grow older, both kinds of men may feel that they should get more from life and seek ways to do so.

Women have a need to respect themselves as individuals, as wives, mothers, employees or employers, wage-earners, but not necessarily in that order. For them, too, the rules keep changing. A woman who was brought up to be a wife and mother may find that she is neither, or that she is both, but in the latter case her children—and the larger society—are unimpressed with these achievements.

Children also have problems of coping with drastic changes, but for them the demands and their responses to the demands come faster and change oftener as they grow and change. And these problems relate not only to members of the nuclear family. Those faced by grandparents, in-laws, siblings, aunts and uncles are equally bewildering

Such discontinuities and role confusions are obvious in white middle-class America, but they are equally important in poverty areas, and especially black poverty areas. A stereotype of black matriarchal society has been accepted as a basic difference, though recent studies have indicated that in many black families a strong, authoritative father is the norm. Strong mothers have been forced into the role because of poverty, or the father's lack of education, rather than because of race. If black women have been better able to get the available jobs than black men, the reason seems to be the faulty organization of the larger system rather than any intrinsic difference in black and white culture.

Chicano families have been described by quite a different set of stereotypes, including such ideas as "family-centered," "familistic," "extended family," "paternalistic," and "male dominated." In "The Chicano Family: A Review of Research," by Miguel Montiel, some of the sweeping generalizations have been discounted and others tempered. Montiel's conclusion seems to be that Chicano families, like most others in our culture, are in the process of change, that broad generalizations about them are likely to be invalid, and that, most of all, a focus on pathology rather than diversity and strengths is mistaken.[1]

Of all systems, perhaps the family is the one in which the complex interrelationships are most obvious. Family relationships start earlier and last longer than nearly any other. They are also apt to be the closest, the most demanding, and the most rewarding. It is not surprising then, that social workers and other professionals have considered the family worthy of a variety of kinds of intervention.

Efforts at prevention of the worst kinds of family problems have long been made by social workers, psychologists, and home economists, as well as lawyers, doctors and clergymen. Education for parenthood, for money management, for sexual expertise has been attempted both formally and informally. Perhaps some of it has been worthwhile. There is no way to know how many families are still intact as a result of these efforts. Certainly prevention is easier and less expensive than treatment or rehabilitation, and well worth the effort.

Efforts at providing services which the family may need but may be unable to provide for itself have been made by social workers since the days of the friendly visitors. These visitors were well-meaning upper-class men and women who sought to give both goods and services to people less well off, as we saw in chapter 3. Social workers provided food, shelter and clothing for many kinds of families whose own resources were sorely limited. Provision was necessary because of lacks in the here and now. Other resources, such as employment, medical care, and counseling services have also been made available to families in need of them. Because of the nature of family relationships, these services can hardly be proferred to one member of the family without involving some of the others.

All the points made concerning relationships with an individual hold true for relationships between worker and family. Sometimes, the worker does not plan to involve the family, but when he makes a home visit, or an office appointment, he finds that he is talking with the whole family. For example:

The Red Cross home service worker called on the mother of a young sailor whose hand had been accidentally cut off in heavy machinery.

[1] Montiel, Miguel, "The Chicano Family: A Review of Research," *Social Work*, 18, no. 2 (March 1973).

The worker was not looking forward to the interview, but mentally reviewed the words she would use in breaking the news. When she arrived at the home, she found the mother, father, younger brother and fiancée assembled. Realizing nothing could be gained from delay, she told them immediately. As they reacted to the news, they turned to each other for comfort and support. The worker could only feel relieved that she was not the only one with the mother.

The family, then, needs both preventive and provisive services. It also needs rehabilitative services when the family structure or function fails.

Since the early 50s, some psychiatrists, psychologists, sociologists and social workers have emphasized family therapy. Advocates of family therapy see the family as the most important of all systems, and regard individuals as subsystems who are interdependent and symbiotic on each other, and on the family as a unit.

While social work has always been aware of the effect of the family on an individual, the emphasis in family therapy is on the family rather than the individual. In 1956, Murray Bowen, a psychiatrist with the National Institute of Health, studied the families of schizophrenics. He concluded that it was the schizophrenic family that produced schizophrenic children. As a result of his investigation, he observed that "the family is a system in that change in one part of the system is followed by compensatory change on other parts." Later, he stated, "The family is a number of different kinds of systems. It can accurately be designated as a social system, a cultural system, a games system, a communications system, or any of several other designations."[2]

Social workers in family therapy operate in the same sequence of planned change as caseworkers, group workers or community workers. First, someone must feel a need for change, someone must initiate the change, the change relationship must be established, a contract made, and the change begun, generalized and stabilized, and finally the relationship must be terminated. But the process is more complex in that the family, rather than an individual member is the client. In the first phase—recognition of need for change—it is rarely a family recognition by the whole family that all members need help. More likely, one member is the recognized problem, and only after a series of sessions does the family see that all need help.

---

[2] Bowen, Murray, "A Family Concept of Schizophrenia," ed. Don Jackson, *The Etiology of Schizophrenia* (New York: Basic Books, 1960).

Given the basic orientation of the family as the unit in need of help, there are various philosophies as to how the help can best be given. In 1969 the Regional Rehabilitation Research Institute of the University of Washington School of Social Work published the results of an investigation of the family as a unit of study and treatment. This extensive investigation of the literature on family therapy classified three main styles or methods of work with families. They are, psychoanalytic, integrative and communicative-interactive. Like the casework methodologies, each category has its own proponents, who, on the basis of their professional background and experience, defend each category at the expense of the others.[3]

Psychoanalytic approach

Family therapists of the psychoanalytic school operate on the same premises as diagnostic caseworkers of Freudian persuasion. They believe in the need for insight into an unconscious mental life by both client and therapist, and in the predetermined development of the individual. According to this theory, every human being goes through predictable phases of the oral, anal, oedipal, latency, adolescent, and adult periods before reaching maturity.

In the oral stage, the infant learns to satisfy his needs, both sexual and aggressive, through his mouth. The baby cries, sucks, and eventually coos and speaks through his mouth. Food and attention come as a result of exercising his mouth. In the anal stage, the child learns to enjoy the experience of owning or withholding his or her feces. Again this is a way of getting attention from the mother. In the oedipal stage, regarded by some psychoanalysts as the most crucial, the child learns to internalize the position of parents and other family members. He must accept the father as the mother's sex partner, and recognize that the child's position is quite different. By this time, according to Freudian theory, the child is learning to distinguish between his own natural drives and the demands made by others, mainly his parents. He must reconcile his own sexual-aggressive urges, his libido, with the demands of reality as imposed by his parents, who represent his superego.

---

[3] Stein, Joan et al., *The Family as a Unit of Study and Treatment* (Regional Rehabilitation Research Institute, University of Washington, 1969).

When the conflicts brought about by these forces, (libido and super-ego) are not resolved at any stage, the result is neurosis. If the conflicts are satisfactorily resolved, the result is a healthily functioning ego. The latter is the goal of psychoanalytic treatment. Since neuroses always have their roots in childhood, psychoanalysis attempts to uncover material which has been repressed, and therefore relegated to the unconscious. The patient divulges material from his past, through memories, dreams, or free association, and the analyst helps him to understand and work through the previously unresolved conflict. Conflict is not the cause of neurosis; only the lack of resolution of conflict.

The family, especially the mother, is seen as having tremendous impact at each stage in an individual's life and, therefore, the family is seen as a natural starting point for the practice of psychoanalytic therapy. However, the most important emphasis is on the unconscious fantasies of the child, not the family as it really was. Thus the inter-action of the family as it could be observed by a therapist is less important to the psychoanalyst than are the internalized representations as reported by the patient in therapy.

Two of the major proponents of psychoanalytic therapy, Ivan Boszormenyi-Nagy and James L. Framo, wrote the book *Intensive Family Therapy* in which they state their belief that they must distinguish between intensive and supportive therapy.[4] Their preference is for intensive therapy, and this typically involves work by one or more therapists with a family over a period of several years. The emphasis is on the individual's neuroses and their roots in the past.

When the focus is on family communication, attention is given primarily to the psychological level and unconscious communication. Psychoanalytic practitioners vary in their approaches. Some prefer individual interviews, some prefer to intersperse these with family interviews, and some prefer to see groups of unrelated individuals having similar neuroses. What they share is an effort to get at the family's problems through intensive work in the psychological background of each individual. For example:

Mr. Wright called for an appointment with a social worker who had been recommended to him by a co-worker in the bank where Mr. Wright worked. Mr. Wright explained that his family seemed to him

---

[4] Boszormenyi-Nagy, Ivan and Framo, James L., *Intensive Family Therapy: Theoretical and Practical Aspects* (New York: Harper and Row, 1965).

totally lacking in family communication. He rarely saw his two teen-age sons, his wife talked to him about only the most superficial things, and he came home at night too tired to do more than watch television as he ate his dinner, and then go to bed. He made a good salary, provided a good home, and did not think he was getting his money's worth from his family. He wondered if the agency could do anything for him. The worker hoped that the family could be helped, but asked if the Wrights were all interested in doing something about their situation, and suggested that a series of weekly meetings be set up, with various members seen on different days. When he heard that the process would probably take three or four years, Mr. Wright said he thought he should think the matter over.

Do you think the worker should have started the interview differently? Would you see the Wrights' problem as one which would lend itself to psychoanalytic study? Why?

Integrative approach

The integrative approach is an effort to include both the individual and the family in diagnosis and treatment. Its major concept is that of *role*. In every family, different individuals play different roles. In addition to the obvious ones—mother, father, oldest, youngest, daughter, son—individual families specify which members will have conflicting or complementary roles. Helen Perlman, explaining role, says "Role offers a social-functioning focus which embraces people in interaction. . . . Role does not allow us to get lost in personality *per se* . . . most persons know and assess themselves only through their role performance."[5]

Otto Pollack, a sociologist who has written about role theory, says, "Family members are viewed as one another's reciprocal and preferred need-satisfiers. . . ."[6] He sees the family as standing between the individual and the more complex organization of society. Nathan Ackerman, a psychiatrist, sees three levels of phenomena in the interaction between an individual and a group: (1) the structure of the environ-

---

[5] Perlman, Helen H., "The Role Concept and Social Casework: Some Exploration," *Social Service Review*, 25 (Dec. 1961), 371–81, and 36 (March 1962), 17–31.

[6] Pollack, Otto, "A Family Diagnosis Model," *Social Service Review*, 34 (March 1960), 19–32.

ment; (2) interpersonal relationships; (3) the internal organization of personalities. He sees the concept of social role as a bridge between the processes of intrapsychic life and social participation. The purpose of the family, he thinks, is security, survival, sexual union and fulfillment, the care of the young and the aged, the cultivation of bonds of affection and identity, and training for social participation.[7] According to him, breakdown may come at any level of interaction, but his therapeutic approach is primarily to the family unit; the individual and his psyche is secondary. Ackerman and his colleagues wish to include in the family sessions all members of the nuclear family, as well as important grandparents, and even pets. However, they will also see individual members or subgroups when this seems indicated, so that their mode of operation is quite flexible. One problem with this flexibility is that training and education of the therapist is difficult. He must depend on his own personal innovations and be able to assimilate completely the many theories about values, mental health and human growth. Arthur L. Leader, a social worker, suggests that the therapist's intervention must be vigorous and active, as opposed to the psychoanalytic aloofness and lack of involvement. Because some families' interactive patterns are so strong the therapist may be sucked into their patterns and experience the same feelings of hopelessness which they suffer.

Proponents of the integrative approach need broad knowledge and highly developed skills, as well as values which are strong and sure. Just as with individuals, families need support and understanding, and also the benefit of the worker's experience. Schwartz's five central tasks are applicable to work with families. For example:

Mr. Wright came to the family agency by prearranged appointment. He had with him his wife and two sons. Ms. Wright and the boys sat on the sofa in the worker's office. Mr. Wright took a straight chair off to the side. When the worker asked if everyone knew why they had come to the office, Mr. Wright began a fairly detailed explanation of events leading to his call. His wife and sons sat quietly, neither agreeing nor disagreeing. When he finished, the worker asked Ms. Wright if this was the way it seemed to her. She looked startled at being questioned directly and said she guessed so. One of the boys said no one had told him why they were coming. The other boy looked annoyed.

---

[7] Ackerman, Nathan, *The Psychodynamics of Family Life, Diagnosis and Treatment of Family Relationships* (New York: Basic Books, 1958).

What do you think the worker might have guessed about this family in this short time? Why didn't the worker let the father do all the talking for the family? Would you have thought anything about the seating arrangement?

Communicative-interactive approach

Conjoint family therapy is the outstanding example of the communicative-interactive approach. The main concept of this type of therapy is that all family communication involves a multiplicity of messages at one time. Actually, this is true of all communication, in or out of the family. Because communication is so important in this kind of therapy, the therapist tries very early to find out what kinds of messages are being given in a particular family. According to Don Jackson and Virginia Satir, parents are the models for the kind of communication which children give and receive.[8] If parental communication is faulty, it is probably a result of *their* parents having poor communication. This would indicate that communicative-interactive therapy is not so completely concerned with the here and now as it would seem to be.

The second major concept involves the idea of family homeostasis. This is an example of the homeostasis or balance in any system. A change in one part of the system causes a change in other parts. If an individual changes as a result of therapy, the rest of the family will change—change, not necessarily improve. The only way to replace the lost homeostasis is with a new, more satisfactory balance. Because so much dysfunctional behavior is bound up with double messages, according to this theory, the therapist's job is to serve as a model for good communication. First, the therapist must clarify the communication between family members, and then send the therapist's messages clearly. Unfortunately, the family may not appreciate having defenses broken down; particularly they may not like having the onus removed from the "problem member," whom Satir calls the "identified patient."[9]

The therapist takes a rather strong position, getting information from each member of the family to recognize the kinds of interaction in

---

[8] Stein, *The Family*, p. 49.

[9] Satir, Virginia, *Conjoint Family Therapy* (Palo Alto, Ca.: Science and Behavior Books, 1968).

this particular family and then making direct suggestions for change. For example, members of the family may not speak *for* each other or *about* each other. They may speak *to* each other.

This approach to family therapy is readily learned by members of various professions: social workers, psychologists, communications analysts and doctors, among others. According to its proponents, basic changes in family communications can take place in a matter of a few months. For example:

The Wright family filed into the interviewing room. As his wife and sons seated themselves, Mr. Wright launched into an explanation of the behavior of his younger son which had brought the family to the office. Jack had been reported by his school as a truant, and there was some suspicion that he had been pilfering change from the school milk fund. Mr. Wright expressed his anger and disappointment with Jack, saying that the boy never appreciated all his father did for him. The worker turned to Jack, asking for his version of the story. Ms. Wright answered that Jack never seemed to care for the family or their worry about him. The worker again asked Jack how it seemed to him. Jack said his parents had already told the story. The worker said she would like to hear how Jack felt. With tears in his eyes, Jack began to explain.

In this example, who is the identified patient? Do you think the worker knew enough about the problem to ask Jack immediately for his story? How do you think the rest of the family would react to this?

Compared with social casework, family therapy is a new way of trying to help people. Its methods are not too different from casework methods, and the basic knowledge, skills and values of all social work are vitally important in working with families. Some of family therapy is used by many caseworkers, and family therapists practice some casework.

Where families are intact, working with the family is desirable and helpful. Unfortunately, many families are not intact. Many individuals have no families, or no families with whom they interact. Even the most enthusiastic proponent of family therapy recognizes that the family is only one of innumerable systems encountered by an individual, and that in some cases, the family is not there at all. Still, if family therapy is not a solution to all social problems, it is one more way of looking at and attacking some social problems. An excellent casebook for family therapy is *Techniques of Family Therapy*, by Jay Haley and Lynn Hoffman.

Summary

Social work with families is closely related to casework, but is also closely related to family therapy as carried on by members of other helping professions, including psychiatry and psychology. Family therapy focuses on the family as a system, and proposes the thesis that healthy families produce healthy individuals, and vice versa. Like casework, family therapy uses different methods, and the proponents of each method, on the basis of their own background and experience, defend that method against all others.

6

Social work with groups

Social casework and social work with families are alike in that they deal with people in already existing relationships. Both these methods recognize the importance of the group to an individual. Belonging to a group is an integral part of life for most people. Sociologists and psychologists have studied the group; and social workers have specialized in this method of working with people.

Group work models

A group can be defined very simply as two or more individuals who have something in common and who interact with each other. Sociologists have classified groups as *primary* and *secondary*. A primary group is one in which members have a face-to-face relationship. A secondary group is one in which the members have only intermittent contacts, and an impersonal relationship. Michael Olmsted, author of *The Small Group* says,

> . . . a group, then, may be defined as a plurality of individuals who are in contact with one another, who take one another into account, and who are aware of some significant commonality.
>
> An essential feature of a group is that its members have something in common and that they believe that what they have in common makes a difference.[1]

---

1 Olmsted, Michael, *The Small Group* (New York: Random House, 1959), p. 21.

He says the term *small group* is "a neutral, indeed a colorless one—it does not prejudge whether the group in question is operating as a primary or a secondary one."[2] Primary groups are usually small, but small groups are not always primary.

The obvious example of a primary group is the family, which fills the qualification of being face to face, and sharing something in common. Many families, however, are not primary groups, for various reasons having to do with time, geographical distance, or lack of interest.

If a natural group, such as a family, is not necessarily a primary group, the corollary is true. It is possible to create a primary group for a specific purpose. It is possible to bring together a group of people with similar needs or problems, and to involve them with each other so that they recognize each other as significant, important people. This is what social group workers do. Sometimes the group worker, as an agent of the agency, forms the group. Sometimes, the group forms itself for its own purpose. Sometimes, the group is formed as a combined effort by the individuals involved and the agency.

Social workers recognize at least three models of group work. Papell and Rothman, in their article, "Social Group Work Models: Possession and Heritage," list social goals, remedial and reciprocal models.[3]

Social goals model

Early group work, like early casework, emphasized a strong direction on the part of the worker and a strong feeling that the worker—or the agency as represented by the worker—knew the right answers. Early group work agencies included neighborhood houses, settlements, the YMCA, Girl Scouts and Boy Scouts. All of these agencies shared the purpose of making better citizens of the members. Settlement and neighborhood houses were instituted in areas where the poor, and particularly the immigrant poor, lived. The agency provided a haven from the very bad housing, but more than that, it provided an opportunity for people to learn along with their friends and neighbors some of the accepted ways of behaving in a new country. This character-

---

[2] Ibid., p. 23.

[3] Papell, Catherine and Rothman, Beulah, "Social Group Work Models: Possession and Heritage," *Journal of Education for Social Work* (Fall 1966), p. 66.

building effort was similar to that of the early caseworkers who gave advice to individuals and families, who were presumed to receive it gratefully. Neighborhood and settlement houses met a real need, and in many places they are still meeting the need to help individuals to adjust to a new system through groups of people like themselves. The group acted as a link between the individual and larger community. In the early days, the larger community was seen to be "right," and learning and adjusting had to be done mainly by the individual with the assistance of the agency. At the same time that these people were learning to work together, they were becoming socially active. They were able to affect factory working conditions and the political process in their wards, thus changing the larger system. Citizen education and social reform were thus seen as two important results of the settlement movement. The degree to which these results became reality depended to some extent on the degree of involvement by the group, the knowledge and skills of the group leader, and the type of cause on which they chose to work. All settlement groups were not successful, but many served to dispel the alienation of immigrant or other such groups.

Girl Scouts and Boy Scouts had much the same purpose, as did the public schools. The group, or the troop, or the class was formed to further the aims of the larger society. Group pressure was found to be a valuable aid to authority, whether of society, school, or agency. If you think of your own experience, you will recognize that many of the people who have been effective in socializing you have been members of your peer group, not parents or teachers. The earliest kind of group work, then, espoused *social goals* as its purpose. This is a purpose which still holds today. The number of clubs, groups and troops have proliferated steadily, attracting more and more members of all ages, sexes and interests. Among early social workers who wrote and practiced group work of this kind were Gisela Konopka, Grace Coyle and Gertrude Wilson. They saw the worker's role as that of enabler or teacher. According to Catherine Papell and Beulah Rothman, the key concepts of social goals are social consciousness and social responsibility.

As previously stated, social goals were the first to be considered in the practice of group work. Group work was recognized as a reasonable way of achieving those goals, not only by social workers but by recreation workers and teachers as well. According to Papell and Rothman,

> . . . a serious shortcoming of the social goals model is that it has not produced a theoretical design that is adequate to meet the problems

facing practitioners in all areas of service. Its under-emphasis on individual dynamics and its lack of attention to a wide range of individual needs leave the practitioner without guidelines for carrying out a social work function with client groups where individual problems take precedence over societal problems. It is difficult to see how this model would serve (except by distortion) to provide a basis for social group work practice with *admission* or *discharge* groups in a mental hospital.[4]

Even the public schools, with their emphasis on grading and conformity have not been successful in molding all kinds of children into the exemplary citizens hoped for by parents and teachers. Rules and regulations appeal to some, but not all, children. The efforts of group leaders and teachers are in no way to be denigrated, but some other methods must be recognized, in dealing with all kinds of people. For example:

The boy's club meeting was late getting started because Fred and Jim did not come in from the playground, but continued their game. John, the president, called the meeting to order, but Fred had not appeared to take minutes. Bill, a younger member, suggested that the group impose a fine on members who came late to meetings. A vote was taken, and passed, seven to three. When Fred and Jim came running into the room, they were informed that they must pay a 10¢ fine. Jim flushed and said angrily that it wasn't fair to vote before he and Fred came in—the others knew they were coming. The group leader pointed out that they knew when the meeting began, and that the majority of those present had agreed on a fine. Jim said he would not be part of such a crooked club. He was resigning. He stalked out.

Do you see the group leader in a very strong position? Do you think he was a social worker? How could the situation have been handled? Did you ever have a similar experience, as a member of a group? How did you feel about it?

Remedial model

Group work with a treatment emphasis follows a remedial model. Someone needs a remedy for something not quite right, and the group worker sets out to remedy the situation. This model is closely associated with the casework method. The treatment of the individual is seen as the most important goal. Fritz Redl, a psychiatrist, pioneered in the

---

[4] Ibid., p. 70.

group treatment of institutionalized children. Robert Vinter is the social worker who is recognized as the leading theoretician for this model. Both Redl and Vinter are concerned with the process of forming the group. Group formation is the first stage in this type of planned change. The worker selects group members whom he sees as most likely to fit into a group because of their age, sex, interest, or problem. As the person who forms the group, the worker knows something of the background of each prospective group member, and relies on his or her professional judgement as to who should be in the group. The worker's role is that of expert and change agent rather than enabler or mediator. According to Arthur Blum,

> A "good" group is the group which permits and fosters the growth of its members. This does not presuppose any fixed structure or level of function as being desirable except as it affects the members. . . . Evaluation of the desirability of its [the group's] structure and processes can only be made in relation to the desirability of its effects upon the members and the potential it provides for the worker's information.[5]

With this emphasis, the term remedial is readily understood. The group is to serve as a remedy for the various members of it. Konopka says:

> . . . the group worker is neither "permissive" nor authoritarian-directive. Acceptance and limit-setting are not considered contradictory in the use of the group work method, but are used according to the assessment of the group members' needs and the situation in which they find themselves.[6]

But acceptance and limit-setting assume a knowledge of and skill in what to accept and where to set limits. In all kinds of group therapy, the worker must emphasize his knowledge and his concern for each person in the group. According to Papell and Rothman, the group leader

> . . . uses a problem-solving approach. . . . He is characteristically directive and assumes a position of clinical preeminence and authority. . . . While his authority must be confirmed by the group, it is not fundamentally established by the group. From this position of authority his intervention may be designed to do *for* the client, as well as *with* the client. The model does not require the worker to give priority to the

---

[5] Blum, Arthur, "The Social Group Work Method: One View," in *A Conceptual Framework for the Teaching of the Social Group Work Method in the Classroom* (New York: Council on Social Work Education, 1958), p. 12.

[6] Konopka, Gisela, *Social Groupwork: A Helping Process* (Englewood Cliffs, N.J.: Prentice-Hall, 1963), p. 111.

establishment of group autonomy nor to the perpetuation of the group as a self-help system.[7]

The worker is clearly the expert.

Because of the heavy emphasis on the individual, much of the worker's expert knowledge is in the areas of individual psychology and treatment. The remedial model emphasizes "treatment goals" as diagnosed, assessed and planned by the worker—not the group.

Vinter has outlined the following principles for social work practice.

1. Specific treatment goals must be established for each member of the client group.
2. The worker attempts to define group purposes so that they are consistent with the several treatment goals established for the individual members.
3. The worker helps the group to develop that system of norms and values which is in accord with the worker's treatment goals.
4. The worker prestructures the content for group sessions based on the worker's knowledge of individuals expressed through his treatment goals as well as his knowledge of structural characteristics and processes that take place within the group.[8]

The remedial group worker, then, forms the group or initiates the change, though the client or some third person may have been the one to feel the need for change. In the other steps of planned change—that is, establishing the relationship, examining alternatives, putting the change behavior into action—the worker is the main figure. The group is seen as the tool for bringing change about. What sorts of groups lend themselves to this directive, authoritarian treatment? As Papell and Rothman suggest, mental hospital patients are one example. According to Papell and Rothman, too:

> . . . the remedial model seems to require a structured institutional context. It assumes clearly defined agency policy in support of treatment goals . . . the remedial model makes less provision for adapting service to the informal life style of the client. It appears to depart from the tradition that the group worker engages with people where he finds them as they go about the business of daily living.[9]

For example, Dr. Jones looked straight at Gary. "Do you want us to believe that you honestly didn't know the other guys in the car were

---

[7] Papell and Rothman, "Social Group Work Models," p. 7.

[8] Vinter, Robert, *The Essential Components of Social Group Work Practice* (Ann Arbor, Mich.: University of Michigan School of Social Work, 1955), pp. 4, 6, 12.

[9] Papell and Rothman, "Social Group Models."

smoking pot when you got in?" Several members of the group groaned. "We can't help you much if you don't level with us, can we group?" Other members of the group nodded. When Gary spoke, it was to Dr. Jones.

If the social goals model emphasizes the importance of the individual conforming to the larger society, the remedial model emphasizes and uses the group to further the goals of the individual.

Reciprocal model

The third model described by Papell and Rothman is called reciprocal because it assumes a reciprocal relationship between the group and the individual. This is the model described by William Schwartz as the mediating model. According to this theory, the individual and the group are interdependent and the worker is the mediator, not only between the individual and the group, but between the small group and the larger group or community. In the worker's role of mediator, the client is seen as neither the individual nor the group nor society but as a dynamic interaction among all three. Schwartz describes this as:

> . . . a relationship between the individual and his nurturing group which we would describe as "symbiotic," each needing the other for his own life and growth, and each reaching out to the other with all the strength it can command at a given moment.[10]

Schwartz proposes that the social worker avoid seeking his identification from either the needs of the individual or society. Instead, his professional identification would derive from the point at which these two sets of needs converge.

This view of the worker's role is more analagous with our view of social systems than either of the earlier models. The worker who identifies with neither society nor the individual, but tries to see both in their context at a given time has a broad view of the system. According to Papell and Rothman,

> . . . the reciprocal model has no therapeutic ends, no political or social change problems, to which it is addressed. It is only from the encounter of the individuals that compose a reciprocal group system that direction

---

[10] Schwartz, William, "The Social Worker in the Group," *Social Welfare Forum* (1961), p. 155.

or problem is determined. Emphasis is placed on engagement in the process of interpersonal relations. It is from this state of involvement that members may call upon each other in their own or a common cause.[11]

In practice, this means to the group worker that the goals which individuals have for themselves become one with the group goals, and that neither of these is set or determined by the worker, whose job is that of mediator. Instead, the group process works to keep worker, individual, group, in step with each other.

Schwartz has given useful listings of the practical tasks with which the mediating worker must cope. They are:

1. The task of searching out the common ground between the client's perception of his own need and the aspects of social demand with which he is faced.

2. The task of detecting and challenging the obstacles which obscure the common ground and frustrate the efforts of people to identify their own self-interest with that of their "significant others."

3. The task of contributing data—ideas, facts, and value-concepts— which are not available to the client and which may prove useful to him in attempting to cope with that part of social reality which is involved in the problems on which he is working.

4. The task of "lending a vision" to the client in which the worker both reveals himself as one whose own hopes and aspirations are strongly invested in the interaction between people and society and projects a deep feeling for that which represents individual well-being and the social good.

5. The task of defining the requirements and the limits of the situation in which the client-worker system is set. These rules and boundaries establish the context for the "working contract" which binds the client and the agency to each other and which creates the conditions under which both client and worker assume their respective functions.[12]

All of these tasks are applicable to the group worker, for whom, indeed, they were outlined. The emphasis on a systems orientation makes less important the setting, or the kind of group composition, than does the emphasis in either the social goals or the remedial models. The important concept in this model is the here and now, and the various systems who are involved with that group. There are numerous examples, of course. Here is one:

---

[11] Papell and Rothman, "Social Group Work Models," p. 10.
[12] Schwartz, "The Social Worker," p. 157.

As the ladies trooped into the dayroom, some of them smiled and spoke to the worker; others did not. Some of them greeted others; some did not. Their average age was 69 years. All of them lived in a four-block area, but they were not neighbors in a neighborly sense. When they had seated themselves, the worker began to speak, telling them how pleased she was to see so many there. She did not mention that twice as many had been invited. She explained that since so many people enjoyed meals on wheels, the agency had thought that perhaps they would enjoy each other's company, or would like to get together occasionally to talk over problems. The agency was concerned about other things than meals, and hoped that the ladies would see some purpose in getting together. A large, white-haired woman said that she thought the meeting was for the purpose of discussing how to lower the cost of the meals. That was what she had come for. Another woman said she thought the group should discuss the question of late meals and incompetent volunteers. At this point, several women spoke at once, both agreeing and contradicting. The worker, raising her voice slightly, explained that the agency had not seen this as the point of the meeting but since there was so much interest, perhaps this would be a good starting point.

Which of the five tasks can you see in practice in this example? At which stage of the change process do you see this group? What factors in group composition seem important? What do you think the group leader was trying to do? What do you think she should be doing?

With regard to social group work models, we can say that the social goals model seeks the good of the group; the remedial model seeks the good of the individual; the reciprocal model seeks a reciprocal relationship between group and individual for the good of both. The three models have grown and developed along with the rest of social work. The reciprocal model seems best to embody social work as it is practiced today and to lend itself best to a systems orientation, but there are still many agencies and many workers whose philosophy reflects both the social goals and the remedial models.

Group work techniques

It is important to recognize that differences in philosophy do not change the process of planned change. Whether dealing with groups, families, or individuals, the worker moves through the same stages. In working with groups, the worker may find that the group is already formed, and then moves on to the first step in forming a relationship. This is particularly likely to be true when a worker takes over a group from another worker or begins work with a natural group. The film *Boy with a Knife* depicts a young worker who hangs around a hot dog stand with a gang of boys until they learn—eventually—that he can be trusted.

The relationship established is more involved with a group, because it is not a one-to-one relationship but involves worker-group member, as well as group members, with each other. Considerable study has been made of group dynamics. Cartwright and Zander point out that groups are "inevitable and ubiquitous,"[13] that they produce dependence, attraction and acceptance, but that they also produce dissonances among members. For the worker, these group properties mean that his knowledge, skills and values must work together to seek out the aspects of relationship which will be useful to each member as well as those which will be most useful to the group and to society as a whole. Establishing a group relationship is as important as—and even more dynamic than—establishing a relationship with an individual or a family. Working toward change also requires that the worker be clear as to what change is sought by the group, by individuals and by the agency, and that he or she knows how to keep the group working on these goals.

Lawrence Shulman has made concrete suggestions for implementing the five central tasks. First of all, he suggests that there are two categories of techniques used by the worker in carrying out his tasks. Cognitive techniques involve *knowing;* transitive techniques involve *doing* to someone or something. Secondly, he lists cognitive techniques,[14] as follows:

> 1. *Identifying the common ground*—The worker must *know*, in his own mind, what common ground exists between the client's or the group's perception of reality, and his or his agency's. In the above example of the elderly ladies' group, the worker accepted goal suggestions which had not originally been part of the plan. In a court-required group, the leader might have had to be much more directive, and much more firm in interpreting the goals of the group.
> 2. *Identifying obstacles*—The worker must *know*, in his own mind, what obstacles are real and which exist only in the perception of group

---

[13] Cartwright, Dorwin and Zander, Alvin, *Group Dynamics: Research and Theory* (New York: Row, Peterson, 1953), Chapter 1.

[14] Shulman, Lawrence, *A Casebook of Social Work with Groups: The Mediating Model* (New York: Council on Social Work Education, 1968), p. 78.

members. Groups may suggest all kinds of reasons why they cannot meet regularly. The worker must be able to sort out the real from the unreal.

3. *Interpreting clues of verbal language*—Interpreting is a cognitive process which the leader uses for his own purpose. The term "old woman" used by one group member to another, may mean denigration, endearment, or merely that the members do not yet know each other's names. The leader must be able to interpret.

4. *Interpreting clues of non-verbal language*—Clues of non-verbal language are observable by a trained worker who works toward learning what clues mean. What, for example, does a group member mean when he turns his back on the person speaking? What does it mean when a member drums his fingers on the arm of his chair? What does a yawn mean?

5. *Identifying patterns of behavior*—Patterns of behavior can be identified only after some time. Individuals and groups eventually show some patterning which may be observed and categorized by the worker. Does one group member take umbrage at another member, regardless of the topic? Does one member always agree with the worker? Does another never agree with the worker?

6. *Contacting one's own feelings*—Contacting one's own feelings requires the worker to notice his own reactions in the same way that he has noted and observed those of the group members. When the client or group member uses bad grammar, does the worker feel uncomfortable? How does he or she feel when the client says "nigger" or "honky"?

All of these techniques involve the worker's thoughts rather than his actions with the group member. They are more nearly related to the worker's values and knowledge than to his skills. Just as the caseworker observes and interprets the nonverbal clues of his client, so the group worker observes and interprets nonverbal clues of each group member, and also of the group interaction. Cognition requires reflection and must precede the employment of transitive techniques.

Transitive techniques involve communications and problem-solving help. According to Shulman,[15] communications include:

1. *Stepping up weak signal*—What is a signal? When a group member says "Yes, but . . . ," and lets his voice drop, the worker may say, "But what?"

2. *Stepping down strong signal*—When a group member shouts, "I hate you," to another group member, the worker may interpose with, "You sound pretty upset," or "What are you so mad about?" What might the worker say if the outburst is addressed to him or her?

3. *Redirecting transaction to actual intended recipient*—Frequently

---

[15] Ibid., p. 77.

group members address the worker when the message is really intended for another member. "Jack always comes late," might get the response from the worker, "Why not tell Jack?"

4. *Reaching for facts*—Reaching for facts involves the worker in asking for factual rather than feeling material. "I can't stand the way my Mother looks at me," might produce questions from the worker as to when, where, and on what occasions the looks occurred.

5. *Focused listening*—Focused listening filters out the extraneous material or cuts short lengthy descriptions. It may also concentrate on feelings rather than information. The mother who says, "I slapped my baby three times last Thursday—or was it Tuesday" is not really concerned about which day of the week it was.

6. *Reaching for feelings*—Reaching for feelings applies to the same type of effort as the above example. The worker may say, "How did you feel after you had slapped your baby?"

7. *Waiting out feelings*—If the mother in the above example hesitates, the worker may wait till she can express her feelings in her own way, rather than prompt or suggest.

8. *Getting with the client's feelings*—The worker may tell the mother, "I can see that you felt pretty bad about what happened."

9. *Sharing your own feelings*—The worker may say to a disgruntled group member, "I have times when I don't feel like coming too," or even, "I would rather have stayed home today too."

10. *Seeking out empathic help*—The worker asks other members of the group to empathize and support the member who is having a hard time getting out his feelings. Or the worker may observe a member who looks sympathetic, and simply ask how he feels.

All of these techniques involve speaking to and hearing out group members. Can you give examples of each of these techniques as you have observed or participated in groups? Skill is combined with knowledge and values in communication, and communication must precede problem-solving help. According to Shulman, "the activity taking place within the group may be viewed as an intricate process of problem-solving, with each member and the group as a whole continuously faced with a series of tasks. . . ." It is the difficulty encountered in problem-solving which calls for the help of a worker. His task, separate and distinct from those of the members, is to serve as a "catalyst" and a "resource" for their problem-solving efforts. Schulman's techniques[16] which follow are movements through which this help is offered.

1. *Providing working data*—The worker knows something that the group members do not. He has knowledge of resources, laws, or other factual data, which he shares with the group.

---

[16] Ibid., p. 78.

2. *Confronting with contradictory reality*—Reality may not always be comfortable or convenient to face. The group may prefer to fantasize about what might have been or what they would like. The worker must confront them with the real situation before they get too carried away.

3. *Pointing out obstacles*—The obstacles which the worker recognized to himself must be shared with the group so that they can work productively.

4. *Pointing out the common ground*—The common ground, previously identified by the worker to himself, must be pointed out to the group. "The agency agrees that you need to work toward a better recreational program for this group."

5. *Defining limits*—The worker explains that no one may leave the meeting room before 9:00 P.M., even though some groups have more flexible meeting times.

6. *Defining contract*—Once the group has come to some decisions about what it will do, and what the worker will do, the worker lists the conditions.

7. *Partializing the problem*—Complex problems can usually be broken down into two or more parts. The worker must be able to take the lead in this breaking down.

8. *Making the problem the group's*—Problems of the individual remain his or hers unless the worker involves the rest of the group in the solving process.

9. *Waiting out the problem*—A group member may be unable to bring up what is bothering him but may talk of other things until he works up his courage.

10. *Offering alternatives*—A group member, or even the whole group may need alternate suggestions when they reach what seems to them an impasse.

11. *Helping the client to see his problem in a new way*—Constant mulling over the problem may have made the group member or the group unable to see different aspects or different ways of looking at the problem.

All of these techniques are closely related to cognition and communication. They are as useful with a single client as with a group, and they are part of the planned change process. Further, they are useful with both task and growth groups.

Task and growth groups

Some social workers, beginning with Gertrude Wilson, distinguish between groups whose main purpose is individual growth and those whose main purpose is the accomplishment of tasks. As in the three previously described models, the difference is one of philosophy rather than of technique.

The use of "growth groups" is a relatively recent development. In these groups, people who are not in need of therapy but think they could benefit from group experience meet with a leader who tries to help them increase their self-awareness, sensitivity to others, and general ability to see themselves through the eyes of others. The group is a useful tool for this kind of understanding, and while sensitivity groups have been abused and misused, there is clearly a great deal to be learned through them. That some people need them is fairly obvious, as is the need for trained professional leadership. The leader's knowledge of group tasks and techniques do not change in growth groups. The planned change process is again the method employed to move the group toward its goal.

Task groups are more nearly related to the practice of community work, which will be addressed in the next chapter. Task groups are formed for the purpose of accomplishing a joint goal for a broad purpose. Examples of task groups are committees, clubs, boards of directors, and even governing bodies. The group is formed to accomplish something; when the task is completed the group may disperse or may move on to another task. Each individual has a role to play and a job to do. Nevertheless, the group leader, who may be called a *chairman* or a *consultant*, must concentrate on the promotion of the planned change process and on an awareness of the various systems which are involved in the working of the group. He must keep in mind the central tasks and the cognitive and transitive techniques which he uses to keep the group at work on its task. The fact that the work has implications outside the individuals in the group does not mean that their individual behavior is unimportant or that their interaction with each other will not matter. Worthy causes will not make up for lack of cooperation on the part of participants. The group leader bears the responsibility for keeping the group at work on its task.

There is considerable similarity between growth groups and therapy groups, except that the leader's role is more reciprocal in the growth group—and the participants would hardly see themselves as in need of remedy. There is considerable similarity between task groups and social goals groups, except that the role of each member of the task group must be recognized as important to the group. And the group's ability to achieve its task is seen as important to the well-being of each member. Thus, both growth and task groups seem to have reciprocal ends—to seek goals for individuals, for groups and for the community at large.

Gerard Egan in his book *Face to Face* describes growth groups as *laboratory learning:*

> The participants come together in small, face-to-face groups in order to interact with and receive feedback from one another in ways that have been proved to develop a variety of human relations skills. Each member, by reflecting on his own behavior and by means of the feedback he receives from the other members, has the opportunity to get a feeling for ("diagnose"), experiment with, and improve his interactional or human-relations style.[17]

Growth groups are also known as *sensitivity, encounter,* or *T* (training) groups. The two best known types of growth groups are encounter and T groups. While the two terms are used interchangeably, there is a difference. Encounter groups typically have no institutional backing, are unstructured and are apt to be led by an untrained leader. They rely more on physical contact and nonverbal exercises, and emphasize an experience, rather than a change, per se.

The T group started with Kurt Lewin, a German psychologist well known for his work in field theory, who emphasized feedback, interpersonal honesty, self-disclosure, unfreezing and observant participation. The leader or trainer is concerned with the group's ability to learn and change, but sees them as functioning individuals who want to grow. The group members see the trainer as someone with more skills and knowledge, but not necessarily more prestige. They expect the leader to participate and they expect to model themselves on the leader. The T group nearly always has a predictable termination point, all members terminating at one time.

T groups are sometimes confused with psychotherapy groups or remedial groups, and there are commonalities between the two. Both groups seek to bring about hoped for change. Both value self-disclosure on the part of the members. Both seek goals above and beyond individual goals, though these are more important in T groups. The differences within the group models may be greater than the differences between them. Some T groups appear to be quite therapeutic, while some therapy groups appear to be supportive and freeing rather than remedial. In general, though, psychotherapy groups are usually smaller,

---

[17] Egan, Gerard, *Face to Face* (Monterey, Ca.: Brooks/Cole, 1973), p. 6.

meet over a long period, and involve serious attention to the problems being considered. T groups may have 12 to 16 members who may spend a great deal of time together for short periods, a weekend or a week. Generally T groups enjoy their meetings, and have fun. The psychotherapy leader is an expert and a professional, both in his own view and in the way the group views the leader. Psychotherapy group members are very aware of their own dysfunctioning, and seek a leader who is omniscient. T group members, then, in general are well-functioning individuals who seek growth; therapy group members find it difficult to cope with everyday stresses, and seek relief, first through their leader and eventually through the group.[18]

While some of these groups operate without leaders, social workers see themselves as participant leaders, perhaps models for other members of the group, but not teacher-experts ready with a diagnosis for each member. Since growth groups propose to enrich and expand individuals' self-awareness and sensitivity to others, they are somewhat like therapy groups, but since the members are healthy, functional people, therapy or remedy can hardly be their purpose. Take the following as an example:

The group were already assembled when the faculty member-leader arrived. Since the group was a requirement of the program, the leader asked how many of the members would have preferred not to be there. No one spoke up, but one member said, "If I felt that way, I wouldn't say so." The leader accepted this, and suggested that those who wanted to be there, tell what they hoped would come from the group. Members said "I'd like to know how I appear to others," and "I'd like to get to know the rest of the group really well," and "I hope we can be open and honest." The leader commended all these ideas, and suggested that they start by introducing themselves and telling some bit of information which they did not usually include in an introduction. Do you think this was a T group or a therapy group? How would you see the leader behaving in the other type group? How do you think the members would relate to the leader in the other type group? Can you imagine an experience which you might have in either type group?

In his article, "Social Group Work: The Developmental Approach," in the *Encyclopedia of Social Work*, Emmanuel Tropp says:

---

[18] Yalom, Irvin D., *The Theory and Practice of Group Psychotherapy* (New York and London: Basic Books, 1970), chap. 14.

Society has moved into a period when people are seeking the human sustenance that has been lost in the course of technological development, . . . and the generally increased complexity and depersonalization of societal structures. The search is for a new sense of community, with intimate and supportive human ties, giving larger meaning to individual lives through significant common purposes. To accomplish these ends, more and more people are finding for themselves their own microcosms of community. There are action groups to re-establish individual ability to make an impact on societal institutions; interpersonal exploration groups in which individuals aim to find out who they really are and how they appear to their fellow human beings; and groups to pursue strongly held common interests, such as learning, experiencing, or performing in the worlds of ideas and skills.[19]

Summary

Social group work, like social casework seeks to promote better functioning of people through the planned change process. The three models for social group work are the social goals model, the remedial model and the reciprocal model. The reciprocal model sees the worker in the role of mediator between systems, and adheres most closely to a systems approach to social work. In any model, the worker must bear in mind his five central tasks and must use techniques of cognition, communication and problem-solving. Task groups and growth groups are reciprocal in their efforts on behalf of individual, group and community.

---

[19] Tropp, Emmanuel, "Social Group Work: The Developmental Approach," *Encyclopedia for Social Work*, 2 (New York: National Association for Social Work, 1971), 1251.

7

Social work with communities

According to Roland Warren, "A community is that combination of units and systems which perform the major social functions having locality relevance." He further lists five major functions of community:

1. Production-distribution-consumption.
2. Socialization.
3. Social control.
4. Social participation.
5. Mutual support.[1]

All of these functions have locality reference, but are not necessarily confined to the locality. Also, all of these functions may be performed by some other types of social systems, groups, formal organizations or whole societies.

According to Murray Ross in *Community Organization, Theory, Principles and Practice*, there are at least two kinds of communities. First, a geographic community includes all the people living in a certain geographic area. An Indian village is clearly a community. The people living there are separate from the people in the next community and separate from the people in the surrounding countryside. The same

---

[1] Warren, Roland, *The Community in America*, 2d ed. (Chicago: Rand-McNally, 1972), pp. 9, 10.

is true for all the other kinds of villages known to us throughout history. But as civilization becomes more complex, communities become larger and less clearly defined. A large town or big city may still be defined as a community in one sense, but it also contains a number of smaller communities. Political, economic, social and religious communities are all separate, and at the same time overlapping, even though the members of the community are all from the same geographic area.

Second, a community of interest is made up of people who share an interest or some interests, whether or not they ever see each other. Some examples are a political party, a church, or a professional organization. These people do not see each other regularly, but their concern for a particular subject allows their community.

Whether geographic or interest, the community is made up of people, individuals and groups. Thus, community work for social workers can easily be seen as social work which involves larger numbers of people than either casework or group work. But a systems orientation shows clearly that mere numbers are only the beginning of the complexity. Every individual, and every group relates differently to each other, to the idea of a problem and to the idea of a worker who is expected to do something about the problem. All the knowledge, skills and values of caseworkers and group workers are called into play in community work, as well as many more kinds of knowledge, many more skills and many new values.

History of community work

Community work is both an outgrowth of other social work methods and a starting point for them. A very early nomadic tribe, believing in one deity, claimed to obey an injunction to "Love thy neighbor as thy self." The Judaic-Christian tradition is built on the idea of all mankind as a community which takes into account the welfare of the whole world. Unfortunately, most people are not able to act according to this injunction. It is easier to recognize the connection between ourselves and those who are physically or mentally near to us. In medieval times, villagers gave allegiance to their masters, and masters needed their villages. With the growth of trade and craft, the population became more mobile, and fewer villagers lived and died in the same village, dependent on the same nobles. Some of these mobile citizens became old, ill, or for some reason, incompetent. Away from their own village they might well put undue strain on the resources of another community.

As mentioned in an earlier chapter, the most famous, though not the first of a series of laws aimed at promoting local responsibility for the poor was enacted in England. The law "43 Elizabeth," enacted in 1601, came to be known as the "Elizabethan poor law," and it was considered to be a model for its time, and for centuries later. Three basic principles were assumed: (1) the state is responsible for those unable to care for themselves; (2) the able poor and the unable poor must be differentially viewed and treated; (3) the unit of poor law relief is the parish.[2] The law provided for paupers in their own community, but by 1662, a more stringent Settlement Act was required because beggars still moved about. According to that act, each parish became responsible *only* for those who had legal residence within its bounds, which usually meant residence by birth. Furthermore, those without legal settlement had to be returned to their proper parish, and newcomers were required to post assurance that they would not become public charges.

This beginning of community responsibility worked toward the dilemma in community organization, with which we must still deal. The dilemma is this: Should community intervention stress the delivery of services to individuals, as the poor law proposed, or should community intervention seek to modify those conditions which predispose people to functioning poorly? Should community work be concerned with treatment or reform? Should the view of social welfare be residual or institutional? Most authorities see that both points of view are needed. There is a need for social planning as well as for social development and social action.

Community work models

According to Jack Rothman, a leading writer in community work,

> There appears to be at least three important orientations to deliberate or purposive community change in contemporary American communities, both urban and rural, and overseas. We may best refer to them as approaches or models A, B, and C, although they can roughly be given the appellations respectively of locality development, social planning, and social action.[3]

---

[2] Fink, Arthur E., *The Field of Social Work*, 6th ed. (New York: Holt, Rinehart and Winston, 1974), p. 20.

[3] Rothman, Jack, "Three Models of Community Organization Practice," in *Social Work Practice 1968* (New York: Columbia University Press, 1968). Reprinted in Cox, Fred, et al. (ed.), *Strategies of Community Organization* (Itasca, Ill.: F. E. Peacock, 1970), p. 21.

The three models overlap, and according to Brager and Specht,

> Community organization is a method of intervention whereby individuals, groups, and organizations engage in planned action to influence social problems. It is concerned with the enrichment, development and or change of social institutions and involves two major related processes: planning (that is, identifying problem areas, diagnosing causes, and formulating solutions) and organizing (that is, developing the constituencies and devising the strategies necessary to effect action).[4]

Nevertheless, there is some advantage in discussing the three models, as if they were separate and discrete.

Model A, locality development, is the particular interest of Murray Ross, who wrote *Community Organization, Theory, Principles, and Practice.* He traces the history of community organization from efforts at social reform and points to the alienation of people in today's industrial, urbanized society. He sees contemporary community organization as attempting to develop (1) meaningful functional communities as members of which individual citizens may have some sense of belonging and control over their environment, and (2) a new sense of neighborhood in the large metropolitan area through creation of citizens' councils and other forms of neighborhood organizations.[5] He uses the term *community development* to mean,

> . . . the utilization under one single programme of approaches and techniques which rely upon local communities as units of action and which attempt to combine outside assistance with organized local self-determination and effort, and which correspondingly seek to stimulate local initiative and leadership as the primary instrument of change. . . .[6]

This definition is taken from a U.N. document and relates mainly to locality development in underdeveloped countries. However, the principles of locality development in the United States are the same. Community organization, according to Ross, is:

> The process by which a community identifies its needs or objectives, orders (or ranks), develops the confidence and will work at these needs or objectives, finds the resources (internal and/or external) to deal

---

[4] Brager, George and Specht, Harry, *Community Organizing* (New York and London: Columbia University Press, 1973), pp. 27, 28.

[5] Ross, Murray, *Community Organization: Theory, Principles and Practice,* 2nd ed. (New York: Harper and Row, 1967), p. 6.

[6] Ibid., p. 8.

with these needs and objectives, takes action in respect to them, and in doing so extends and develops cooperative and collaborative attitudes and practices in the community. . . . The result of the community organization process, at any stage, is that the community should be better equipped than at some previous stage, or before the process began, to identify and deal cooperatively and skillfully with its common problems.[7]

This model assumes that it is possible to bring about social change through the participation of a large section of the community. If something is wanted badly enough, so goes this theory, then all members of the community will work together to achieve their goal. While working together, they will heighten their sense of community and take a greater interest in achieving their goal. This is an extension of the social work principle of self-determination. Every community, like every individual and every group, has a right to work toward its own goals; and its work is more likely to be successful if more people rather than fewer people are involved in planning and doing. This model assumes that there is a very democratic makeup in the community. Community organization in early agencies, settlement house programs, and Peace Corps projects followed the theory that everyone would work for the benefit of all. If differences existed, they could be reconciled through rational, democratic discussion. Without this effort at community development, agencies would have gone off on their own bent, meeting needs as they saw them, and overlooking needs they did not see. The idea of cooperation and collaboration has had tremendous effect on the efforts of social work reformers. Community Councils, Community Chests, and councils of social agencies have all tried to proceed in what they conceive to be a democratic way to meet the needs of a community without duplication or neglect. Sometimes, however, agency directors and board members have assumed that their view of the community need was the only one. Their experience and knowledge presumably have made them better able to make decisions about community needs than others in the community. Further, they are the members of the community whose power makes their ideas work. They see the community as a homogeneous entity rather than as a system made up of heterogeneous subsystems.

With this view of the community, what role does the locality developer practitioner play? Usually, he or she is an enabler or mediator or

---

[7] Ibid., pp. 40, 50.

teacher. Since the community is a benign organization, the worker is primarily concerned with coordinating, consulting, or lending a vision to the community leaders. Presumably, he or she works *with* not *for* the community representatives. The worker views the whole community as one. There is no suggestion that powerful figures in the community may have different ends from the welfare of the community. It is conceivable, however, that these powerful people have more influence than some others. It is considered reasonable to cultivate them. For example:

The bimonthly meeting of the board of directors of the local mental health association was called to order by the chairman. His executive secretary, Ms. Poole, sat at his right to take minutes. The main topic for discussion was the plan for a social club for returned mental patients. Ms. Poole had talked with each board member about the plan prior to the meeting. Some of the members who had said they would be at the meeting were not present. The Rev. Black, an old-time resident of Rivertown, seemed to be the outstanding opponent. He opened the discussion by saying flatly that the association could not afford to spend money on such an expensive project when no one knew if it would be used at all. He felt sure that his congregation would resent a special house for mental patients. Ms. Smith, the newest board member, said that, as a former mental patient, she knew the need for a social club in Rivertown was great. She felt that it was a good use for the group's money. The Rev. Black sniffed.

This is the kind of issue with which a locality developer deals. Hopefully, Ms. Poole has some information about costs and use of social clubs in other communities. But the group must have some idea of the acceptability of such a project in this community. Is the Rev. Black a better judge of the community reaction or is Ms. Smith? Is it likely that the community, which funds the Mental Health Association, will approve such a fund use? Ms. Poole will not have a vote on the question, but she will certainly have a voice in the discussion. Besides contributing data, she will be involved in lending a vision of the kind of community which supports a social club. She will also be a buffer between differing factions on the board. Because she believes that all the members have the best interests of the community in mind, she will smooth ruffled feelings, and make sure that everyone's point of view is heard. Ms. Poole will be playing Shulman's "mediating" role. She will be recognizing the individual dignity of each member, and will accept each. Her knowledge of this community, and of others, will come into play with her skill in bringing out all members' ideas, as will her values of democratic discussion and majority rule. She will work toward consensus among all the members, feeling that this group will be stronger and the community better if everyone is satisfied with the vote, however it turns out.

Model B, the social planning approach to community work is oriented toward a problem-solving effort at social reform. Present-day community problems such as health, housing, employment, recreation are seen by Roland Warren, one of the leading proponents of this approach, as being of such great import that they require high-level planning, both for prevention and treatment. Because of their size and complexity, these problems cannot wait for local democratic community processes for solution. Instead, professionally trained experts with a great deal of knowledge not available to the general public must study and work toward solving the problems. In their case book, *Community Organizers and Social Planners,* Joan Ecklein and Armand Lauffer describe the activities of social planners as follows:

> . . . (1) fact finding and problem definition, (2) the building of communication or operating structures, (3) the selection and determination of social goals and policies in the design of action strategies, (4) some aspect of plan implementation, (5) the monitoring of change and assessment of feedback information. . . . Planners are not free agents. They are employed on a regular or consultation basis by organizations and groups. What they actually do, and the problems they attune themselves towards, (sic) are very much the functions of the auspices under which they work.[8]

The role of the worker, then, is that of expert. He must be expert in fact-gathering, in analysis, and in knowing in depth what to do about problems. He must also have knowledge of the particular problem. The planning expert is not an amateur interested in enabling a community to solve problems in their own way. He uses his knowledge at the request of powerful community persons, and is presumably hired by them. He is less concerned about conflict or consensus of interest, since he regards factual material as uncontestable. He sees the client community as consumers of his knowledge and skills. The planner is less oriented to philosophies and practices of social work than his colleague in community development, and more oriented toward research and evaluation,

---

[8] Ecklein, Joan and Lauffer, Armand, *Community Organizers and Social Planners* (New York: John Wiley and Sons, 1972), p. 211.

though he may have a background in traditional social work. For example:

Jack Davis was a social worker who had been hired by the state for the express purpose of developing a program for the employment of mentally retarded citizens. He had an advanced degree in special education for the mentally retarded and he had worked with mentally retarded children in a residential setting. His view of retarded people as citizens with rights and privileges was the result of considerable education and experience. The state legislature's bill calling for a program for the mentally retarded seemed sensible and timely and necessary. Because he could cite national figures regarding the employability of retarded persons, Jack was able to convince some of the legislators that an employment program was in order. Because he knew and understood the general public's fear and misunderstanding of retarded people, he did not rely on a program developed by counties, to be financed by the state. Long conferences with local officials gave Jack a chance to hear their points of view, but he felt no need to give in or to settle for a compromise. He did behave courteously and diplomatically, but he left no doubt that his was the expertise, that he was the paid professional, and that the counties which qualified for state aid must abide by the guidelines laid down by the state.

What differences do you see between the approaches of Jack Davis and Ms. Poole? Do you think that the personality of each is the explanation? Do you think that Jack's method of operating shows that his training is superior to Ms. Poole's? Can you think of a situation in which the two might trade roles?

Model C, social action, illustrated by the work of Saul Alinsky and his Industrial Areas foundation, regards process and planning as one device used by the establishment to forestall needed action. To the social actionists, the problem is always one of redistributing the power relationships in a community and, therefore, of providing goods or services to people in need. They do not see powerful figures as allies or as employers. Their view is that all problems are a direct result of power in the hands of the few to the detriment of the many, resulting in social inequality, social injustice and social deprivation. They see all communities divided into two groups, the *haves* and the *have nots*. The task which they see is to change these groups, at least in some areas. Their procedure is to crystallize issues, determine the target population and take action designed to resolve the issues against the target population. The method they use is one of contest and conflict. Because they feel that they are destined to right a wrong, they see little room for consensus or collaboration or compromise. The practitioner's role is that of activist-advocate, one who sees injustice and allies himself with the oppressed rather than the oppressors. The activist-advocate is involved and partisan, not objective and remote. He is not concerned with democratic process except in his own organization. He is not interested in long-term plans. His concern is with the oppressed segment of a community, and his efforts are directed at the overturn of the oppressors. For example:

Max Gold had had little experience with migrant workers before he came to work with the Miron County welfare department. As he listened to the requests for aid—most of which he could not fill—he became more and more angry at the county-state-federal system which provided elaborate regulations for giving no aid to migrants, who were mainly black, poor, and uneducated. Max asked Joe White, a migrant worker with whom he had become acquainted, if he thought the workers would come to a meeting. Max did not ask his supervisor or his county director. A rather small group showed up, mainly those who could be found that night by Joe. Max began by explaining that migrants are deprived of the rights which are theirs by law, because they had never questioned the regulations. Max wanted to make an example, to hire a lawyer, and make the county and state recognize the responsibility they had to migrants. Most of the people at the meeting shifted uneasily. No one said anything until one man asked timidly who would be the example. Max said Joe had volunteered. Someone else asked what would happen when the company found out. Max said the company probably would be upset. So what? Migrants were working for starvation wages anyway. A black man in the rear pointed out that they might well have no wages if the company were upset. Max asked how many had applied for welfare aid and been turned down. Several raised their hands. Max said they might as well save themselves the trouble of applying. Until they had a clear legal ruling, they would never get aid.

The next morning Max was called into the director's office and told that unless he put a stop to his agitating he would find himself out of a job. Max explained that the meeting had been a lost cause from the beginning. The workers did not want to establish their legal rights.

What is the difference between the approaches of Max and Jack

Davis? Do you think Max's lack of knowledge is the difference between his reception and Jack's? How would Ms. Poole have proceeded in this situation? How would you have proceeded? Why? Do you think migrant workers are different from other community groups? Do you think a migrant community is different from other communities? Do you think Max would have had an easier time if he had been a black migrant worker's son?

Phases of planned change

In community work, as in the other methods of social work, change comes about at the instigation of someone. The community may feel the need—as in the state legislature which responded to constituents' dissatisfaction with current programs for the mentally retarded. Or, it may be an agency worker like Max Gold who sees the injustice in the current welfare system and tries to do something about it. There are also cases where entire agencies perceive injustice and inequality, and some agencies have as their main purpose the attacking of current injustices. Or it may be an entirely different group—outside the community—which sees the need for change and initiates the process. The federal government frequently sets about changing local programs without being requested to do so by the locality.

In any case, once the initiation is under way, the problem must be studied, identified and analyzed by someone. As in the case of the discussion of the mental health association earlier, the study may be partly of facts and figures, partly of feelings and biases and values. The community, like the individual, the family, or the group, must have its own individual analysis. Like the individual, the family, or the group, all communities have something in common, but all have their individual identities as well. These must be observed and evaluated, either formally or informally, by professionals or by members of the community.

Having sized up the situation, some plan must be developed, some proposal for change. In locality development, the plan will include increased participation by members of the community, whatever the plan. In community planning, the problem will receive more attention than the process by which it is achieved, and in social action, the plan will include an effort to strip some power from the establishment and give it to some other group. Social activists feel, among other things, that power is a scarce commodity, which is not shared, but held by a few. These few never give up their power willingly, so they must be relieved of it by pressure. Conflict is a necessary and inevitable attribute of all change, according to the activist.

Stabilization and generalization of the planned change process depends, as in casework and group work, on the success of the first part of the plan. In locality development, the process orientation posits that a successful experience for an involved community group will give them the courage and confidence to try again, either on another plan or on an extension of the current plan. Peace corpsmen who have been able to get the trust of their communities have found that building a successful road, or even a successful chicken coop, can give the community the kind of esprit de corps needed to attempt more difficult and involved projects. Neighborhood workers in large cities have found that picketing or writing a letter to a city official is sometimes encouraging enough to get the community started on another leg of a project. Conversely, the lack of success or lack of cooperation in the first step may well discourage any more efforts on the part of the community as a whole.

Community planners, less concerned with the process of change, feel that the merit of the actual problem-solving plan determines the success of further steps. The better the plan, they say, the more likely it is to work. However, they recognize that lobbying, educating, and publicizing contribute much to the success of excellent plans. A state's youth program that has been well thought out and based on other experience and a thorough knowledge of the needs of this state may fail miserably simply because the legislature approves the program but fails to appropriate enough funds to make it work. Thus, part of the plan must be to convince the legislature that the program must be adequately funded, even at the expense of some other worthwhile programs. Community planners, like social activists sometimes recognize a scarcity of resources and the need to take resources from one group to give to another.

Social action gauges the success in stabilizing and generalizing a plan of change by the amount of involvement, by the goodness of the plan and by the degree to which the opposition has been forced to give up power. Civil rights groups, members of the women's movement, and labor unions recognize that *one* episode, *one* kind of strategy will not change the balance of power in their favor. But they also recognize that a minor success in the beginning stage of their effort will provide encouragement for their own group as well as recognition by the general public and discouragement for their opponents. In systems terms, disequilibrium in any part of a system involves new inputs, processing and feedback in the rest of the system. Social action sees the need for providing some of the disequilibrium, and then providing the means to prevent the new equilibrium being the same as the old.

Finally, termination in community work may not be the same as is disengagement in work with individuals and groups. Some community work is ongoing, only the project changes. Civil rights leaders like Martin Luther King did not see the end of community work for them and their cause. In King's case, his untimely assassination ended his part, but his program has been continued by other leaders. On the other hand, Peace Corps workers and other community workers in developing countries have aimed to get a program underway and then depart, hoping that the community will take responsibility from that time on. The planner also sees the end of one project and turns to another, which may have been engendered by the first. All of these examples assume that the worker makes the decision to terminate, but as in casework and group work, the choice may be out of the hands of the community worker. Sometimes the community terminates a program actively and decisively. They are unhappy with the project or with the worker, or they lose interest and motivation. Sometimes the community terminates by simply losing interest. Tasks are not done, meetings are unattended. One of the reasons for this type of termination comes in the early study and fact-finding stages. A community may decide to find out about the need for day care for children of working mothers in the community. A number of volunteers start conducting a survey. The more they survey, the more complex the problem becomes. After a few months of questionnaires and interviews, the volunteers decide passively that the job is too big and their facts and figures are not very helpful anyway. Bulky reports gather dust in the worker's office while the volunteers look around for a project which will get results quicker. Necessary as fact-finding is, it is all too easy to become so involved in it that it is never used; besides terminating a project too soon, enthusiastic volunteers are turned off without achieving the goal they have sought. What could have been a good experience in community service is a disappointment.

Termination of a project may also be the result of a force outside the community. The cutting off of federal funds was an example of sudden termination of many projects in the early 70s. While most communities and most community workers will try to prevent the immediate effects of such cuts, they recognize that they are dependent on political and economic forces, not only for funds, but for philosophic support as well. In the United States, enthusiasm for the "Great Society," for example, was replaced by enthusiasm for law and order, and both were lost in the concern about inflation.

For whatever reason termination occurs, and whoever brings it about, an important aspect must be an evaluation of the project and its process. Community projects are particularly vulnerable to self-fulfilling prophecies. The supporters think the projects will succeed and the opponents think they will fail. Without some built-in device for measuring, whose ideas will prevail? The commitment to evaluation requires that the project have carefully spelled-out goals and objectives in the beginning and that these be assessed at the end. If the goal is a new traffic light in a busy intersection, is the light installed? Is it promised? Has any progress been made? If so, what kinds of manipulations produced the change? Who was involved? What mistakes were made? If the goal is the passage of a legislative bill for licensing day care, did the bill pass? What held it up? Whose efforts were mainly successful? Whose efforts failed, and why?

Describe a community organization project in which you have been involved, and analyze its progress and process. Did you have an evaluative component? How could you have built one in? Successful termination assumes that evaluation has been completed. Even unsuccessful termination requires evaluation.

Brager and Specht have developed an outline for community organization process, which incorporates the development of an organization from small groups through institutional relations. The types of functions which they describe are:

1. Socialization—the process of teaching individuals the values, expectations and behaviors which the community considers important for them to learn. Usually we think of these in terms of children and their learning, but they are equally applicable when applied to adults in whom some change is desired. The key to socialization is the effort to change the individual members, rather than the society.

2. The formation of affective relationships, or primary groups. The

function seeks to satisfy people's needs for social and emotional closeness with others. The key to primary groups is to bring about some change in the relationships between participants, and to develop a sense of belonging.

3. The organization development function introduces people to others who share their personal, professional, political, or philosophical interests. The main task is to expand the constituency, broaden support and develop new coalitions or organizations.

4. Institutional relations organizations seek to change organizations in the interests of the constituents of community efforts.[9]

All of these functions are a part of the planned change effort, and all seem to be required at some point for the development of a full-fledged institutional relations organization.

Similarities and differences

Like casework and group work models, the three models of community work are more alike than they are different. All three involve work with larger systems than casework, family work or group work. All three use traditional social work knowledge, skills and values and all three require other additional knowledge, skills and values. We have seen that each has different goals and involves different roles, as well as different techniques, and different values.

Charles Grosser in his book, *New Directions in Community Organization*, suggests that, given an institutional orientation rather than the traditional residual view, clients and workers have equal, though different roles. In many settings, including the Social Security Administration, clients contribute, receive benefits, and are sometimes also the dependents of a recipient. The workers are neither enablers nor advocates working on behalf of their clients. Instead, workers and clients work together to make policy. Both workers and clients suffer from dysfunctional social arrangements; both workers and clients need each other to cope with the complex social environment.[10]

Sometimes community work is broken down into neighborhood or grass roots community work and planning. While each of the three

---

[9] Adapted from Brager and Specht, *Community Organizing*, pp. 69–76.

[10] Grosser, Charles, *New Directions in Community Organization* (New York: Praeger Publishers, 1973), pp. 13, 14.

models may have some aspects of both, usually locality development and social action are seen to be more directly related to face-to-face work in neighborhood communities, while community planning is likely to be on a higher level. Still it is accepted that all kinds of community work need planning in order to arrive at any kind of success. It is also accepted that both locality development and social action may be carried on at a high level. The idea of board membership at any level requires democratic process and diplomatic handling. As well as representing the larger community, a board is a task group and, as we saw in the previous chapter, task groups have all the attributes of other groups.

All kinds of community workers must be aware of and understand the funding of their community, their project, and the funding of both larger and smaller groups with whom they may be connected. While this is true to some extent with caseworkers, family workers, and group workers, their familiarity with funding is not quite so vital as it is for workers concerned with planning, development, or social action. The former are not usually the people who make decisions about raising and spending funds. Community planners may have control of large sums for a project. On the other hand, locality developers may spend much of their time working out means for raising even enough funds to buy office stationery and to pay the telephone bill. Social action groups such as the Farm Workers Union must figure out the best way to accomplish a great deal with almost no funds.

Another unique contribution to community work is the extensive use of volunteers. Volunteers are used in casework and family work and group work agencies, but not extensively and only in specific, limited jobs. In community work, volunteers are a vital part of any operation, from top-level planning to stuffing envelopes for sending mailings. Community work is built on and for volunteers. Locality development regards the involvement of all kinds of people as the first priority for success. Social action needs an actively participating group to counter established power. Board membership in planning agencies is frequently made up of volunteers whose expertise is related to the problem at hand.

An example of volunteers in community work is the Community Chest or Council, which seeks to coordinate fund raising, priorities and planning for all the agencies in the community. Members of the board of directors are probably volunteers, powerful men from business or the professions, usually with a token housewife representative. This board decides on the basis of agency presentation which money shall be given to whom and for what purpose. The board then sets a quota to be filled by various fund-raising teams, all volunteers. Publicity for the campaign is arranged through and by volunteers, many of them housewives. In a large city, professional workers may coordinate all these activities, but in a smaller community only the director (assisted by a clerical staff) may be a professional. All other tasks may be done by volunteers.

Working with volunteers requires certain special kinds of knowledge and skills. Volunteers are not clients and they are not paid workers. The rewards which they can expect to receive from volunteer work are subjective and personal. Committed, dedicated volunteers are vital to community work, but one of the prime reasons for losing volunteers can be the lack of interest and concern on the part of the professional worker or workers. Since the 60s, a new type of volunteer, the indigenous worker, has been sought by various agencies. Indigenous workers come from the client group, and presumably can work in ways unknown to professionals because the clients are more likely to trust their own neighbors. The concept is a good one, because indigenous workers are likely to have a commitment to the kind of work being done, and because it is high time that clients were consulted about the kind and amount of service they want. Some projects require client representation on planning and policy boards in order to qualify for funds. Thus, clients and policymakers become one and the same. To perform their best service, these policymakers must have the same status, the same respect as any other policymakers. They may need more support from the professional workers because they recognize their lack of power and are not sure they will be heard. For example:

Silver City's Community Action Program was made up of "community leaders" such as real estate brokers, lawyers, a physician and three business men. In order to qualify for federal funding, they had invited a construction worker to join their group. On the first meeting night, Mr. Smith, the construction worker, who was black, arrived first. He chatted with the social worker, who was the only paid professional on the project. As the other members arrived, the social worker introduced Mr. Smith, who was then ignored. During the discussion of housing problems, the social worker made a special point of asking for Mr. Smith's views and experience. Mr. Smith's technical knowledge of construction problems became clear, and the community leaders listened.

Do you think Mr. Smith should have been one of the original members of the CAP? Why do you think he was not? If you were Mr. Smith, would you have accepted the assignment? Why? What role do you see the social worker playing in this sketch? What other possible roles might the social worker play?

Summary

Community work, like casework, family work, and group work is concerned with people and with social systems. The social systems in a community are larger, but they are still made up of individuals, families and groups. Communities may be geographic or interest, or both, and the social worker who works with communities needs to know about communities in general, and his particular community specifically. There are at least three conceptualizations of work with communities: locality development, social planning and social action. While these overlap, and are sometimes practiced together, each has its own theory, goals, roles, and techniques. Like models in casework, family work, and group work, all use social work knowledge, skills and values, and all make use of the planned change process.

8

Some implications for the future of social work

In looking at history, we saw that a variety of systems affected each other, as well as subsystems and supersystems, to effect changes in the process of social work. From a charity or residual system to a social welfare or institutional system in both the United States and England seems in retrospect to be a very logical, and predictable process. Only with hindsight, however, can this process be determined. When we look at the future it is much more difficult to see either short-range or long-range developments. At the same time we must recognize that the vicissitudes of economics, politics and religion are compounded by their interrelationships with each other, as with new and previously unconsidered changes in ecology, demography and population growth, to mention only a few. Planned change must always recognize the reality that unplanned change is a real part of life.

Nevertheless, we must try to predict some kinds of things in both the short run and the long run, for the sake of practitioners who are already in the field of social work, and for students who wish to know whether or not the field is one in which they are likely to succeed.

First, let us hypothesize that social work is a profession which is likely to be around for some time to come. This seems likely despite what has become known as backlash sentiment in the entire field of social welfare. Social welfare legislation has rarely been repealed, once enacted. The social security laws, long overdue, difficult to administer, and inadequate as they were and are, have not been seriously questioned ever since they were enacted in 1935. Even the most fiscally conservative campaigners in their appeals to irate taxpayers have not suggested that the United States would be better off under a system of voluntary charity for the poor. Old-age insurance, unemployment insurance, and assistance for certain categories of disability, including families of dependent children, are now part of U.S. life. Increases in social security payments, expansion of the regulations to include even limited medical care, a proposal for guaranteed income, have all met with resistance and loud protests of "socialism," but no one has suggested that earlier efforts toward "socialism" be taken away. For whatever reason—religious, economic, or political, or something else—social legislation, once enacted, seems to persist.

The same systems which have been operative in the past in shaping social work will probably continue to be so. How can changes in the religious, economic and political systems be expected to affect social work?

Religion

Two recent changes in the religious system in this country and in England may be expected to have considerable effect on the practice of social work. One is that the religious institutions have recognized that they have functions other than theological ones. Most churches nowadays have extensive programs of recreation, socialization, social welfare and community action. Most churches feel a responsibility to take an active part in the everyday lives of the members, not just their Sunday lives. Middle-class church members have felt a need to go outside their normal church activities, outside their own suburbs. In large measure, they have been urged and encouraged in their social consciences by clergymen of all denominations, many of whom have led the way to community action far removed from pastoral duties. The freedom riders of the early 60s, the Pentagon sit-in in the mid-60s, and the poor people's march in the late 60s had a large component of clergy from all over the country. Thus, in many ways, the churches have led community participation for community action.

The second change in the religious system is that many of the previously accepted norms and values are no longer universally accepted. Marriage and family mores are changing. So are many of the concepts related to law and order. Civil disobedience became acceptable in the 60s, but the 70s have brought such a confusion of public wrongs in high places as to make sit-ins and protests somewhat parochial matters. The whole question of law and order has been replaced by the concept of individual personal responsibility, at least in some circles. The thought of an authority who decides right and wrong, reward and punishment is antithetical to many people, particularly to many young people. Having discarded the need for a deity to take care of them, these people have turned to humanistic values. They feel the need for closer relationships with people. Relationship is a time-honored social work concept which, as Biestek pointed out, involves acceptance, a nonjudgmental attitude, confidentiality, self-determination, individualization, purposeful expression of feeling, and controlled emotional involvement. None of these refers to authority, law-making, or even the Ten Commandments. As more people recognize more need for satisfying relationships, understanding and use of these relationships may become the most important concepts for all people, not just those in the helping professions.

Ironically, the opportunities for satisfying relationships are few and far between.

> Modern industrial society tends to destroy and not to build relationships. Technological developments require shifts in occupation and changes in living environments. There is no identity, or relationship on a personal basis with a monopolized industry, a large company, or the society as a whole, represented by the tax gatherer, and police. There being no relationship, there is no motivation for observing the rules. This is a situation that will get even worse as industrial society gets larger and even more anonymous. The "outsider" and the "dropout" now comprise a growing subculture.
>
> At the same time industrial society makes greater demands on its members, it is competitive, its luxuries become necessities, and its inequalities provide a motivation for types of behavior which defies its property-based norms. Furthermore, our cultural goals include acquisition and success measured by wealth. . . . The two factors, the absence of relationships that if present would promote conformity and the presence of pressures that motivate deviance, together ensure an increasing level of organized crime, for relationships can be developed within a criminal subculture, thus satisfying a basic human need. The norms of this subculture are policed, as in the wider society, by the value its members attach to relationships within it. Thus all its members are required to observe norms of violence against the wider society from which they feel rejected.

This quotation is from an address by Dr. John Burton, Director of the Center for the Analysis of Conflict, University of London, made to the British Association for Social Workers, October 25, 1973. Dr. Burton's thesis is that law and order and institutional norms are in themselves examples of structural violence which individuals are fighting against. Because there is no longer universal acceptance of these norms, people find themselves in greater need than ever of close personal relationships. To give some concrete examples: Marriage and the family are no longer accepted as the only life styles available to people. Alternatives include communal living, unmarried couples living together, and homosexual couples living together. None of these was a public possibility in white middle-class culture ten years ago. Even today legal prohibitions against some or all of them exist in some places. Nevertheless, they are now viable alternatives. People who choose marriage and family are no longer bound by law or by public opinion to stay married for life. Parents are still legally responsible for their children, but *all* parents are not responsible, and increasingly this responsibility is accepted by the state.

Economics

Economically, all countries, including England and the United States, have felt the effect of ever-increasing inflation. In brief, inflation means that money becomes worth less in terms of buying real goods. In times of inflation, the people who suffer most are those on fixed incomes. When these incomes are fixed at a very low level, as with welfare recipients, the suffering is acute. But since the inflation is affecting all sectors of the economy, the government is not likely to remedy the situation by increasing welfare or social security grants. In 1973, with considerable difficulty, the monthly social security payments were increased by 11 percent. Not only was this too little to be helpful to those consumers who most needed relief, but it had to be paid for from increased taxes withheld from the paychecks of workers who already felt the pinch of the inflation. There has been little discussion of the possibility of increasing welfare grants for any of the categories, in spite of the fact that the current grants have been inadequate for years.

Before anything constructive was done about inflation, the nation and the world found themselves plunged into an unprecedented crisis of shortages. All kinds of industries have suffered from lack of oil and natural gas, but more important is the threat of a world-wide food shortage which will affect not only the underdeveloped countries which usually suffer from such problems, but the rich and developed countries as well. Such a shortage is bound to have results which can only be vaguely imagined. Food is taken for granted in much of the world. A lack of it scarcely seems possible. But if it is in short supply, the first to suffer will be those who usually suffer: the old, the poor, the disadvantaged.

Politics

The economic picture would have been dreary enough, in any case, but its impact has been heightened for people on welfare by the conservative, big business orientation of presidential administrations which have held to the notion that rising costs and shortages will eventually right themselves if left alone. The government's concern for business interests rather than consumer interests gives little hope for relief for those consumers who are farthest down the list. Given the government's reluctance to act on behalf of the poor, two possible results may be looked for.

First, the position of very poor people may become so bad as to render them nearly helpless as well as hopeless, and their numbers may become expanded to the point that unemployment is a fact for great numbers of U.S. citizens. As in other times and in other countries, the poor may simply accept their fate and, like the conservative government, wait for times to get better. The second possibility is that this generation of poor people may be unwilling to accept their fate. Experience with some degree of self-determination during the previous decade may encourage them to take a second route. They may organize, demonstrate and protest. Whether or not they can be successful remains to be seen. A frightened and deprived population may react differently to a war on poverty from an affluent society.

Given either of these possible courses of action, what will be the posture of social work? Will social workers line up with the clients or will they feel that their role is that of mediator or broker between the oppressed and the oppressors who are not much better off? No answers can be given. But social work's relatively new position of change agent would seem to indicate that the profession will need to move beyond earlier efforts in times of economic and political recession. If social workers are committed to changing the system and affecting public policy, they will surely not be satisfied with applying band-aids on the worst of the social ills and ignoring the rest.

Values, skills, knowledge

Social work has changed in all three of its basic concepts, since the great depression. At the beginning of the 30s, social work values included not only respect for individual dignity and self-determination, but also acceptance of prevailing moral codes, patriotism, respect for law and order in government, and a general appreciation of capitalistic principles. The social work skill most widely used was casework, with its intrapsychic implications. In the last three decades, group work and community work have increasingly become the methods for bringing about change in direct service to clients. While increasingly more attention has been given to using all three direct methods, indirect methods of working on behalf of clients through government, education and economics have likewise become more widely understood and used. If these additional skills and the knowledge they represent have real and lasting value, it seems likely that social workers will use them in behalf of the clients who need them more than ever before.

Social work's knowledge base has expanded, since the 30s from a psychological, psychoanalytical orientation, through an overwhelming concern and respect for social science orientation, to a confidence in its own ability to use the concepts and concerns of other fields only as they relate to social work.[1] Like other fields of higher education, and like other programs for professional training, social work has had to face the problem of finished product or continuing education. Can students ever finish their educational experience, or should they learn to think in terms of education as a lifelong process? Given the uncertainty of practice goals and settings, the latter seems a more likely occurrence. The Council on Social Work Education has been increasingly concerned with change. In the *Journal of Education for Social Work* for Spring, 1974, Daniel S. Sanders says:

> Increasingly, the demands of a changing society have necessitated a reexamination by the social work profession of its educational goals,

---

[1] Boehm, Werner, *Trends in Higher Education and Future Directions of Education in Social Work*, a paper presented at Session 109, the 20th Annual Program Meeting, Council on Social Work Education, Atlanta, 1974.

perspectives, and modes of intervention. While the profession has responded to the new needs and opportunities posed by a changing society with curriculum innovation, limited attention has been given to a much needed multicultural and pluralistic perspective. The situation of "cultural and professional myopia" persists and is a severely limiting factor in the educational preparation of social workers for effective practice in a pluralistic society that is in the throes of social change.

He describes the dilemma of social workers as follows:

> Social work intervention to meet the demands of a changing society calls for social workers to exercise two roles: that of helping individuals, groups, and communities to cope with the problems resulting from change, for example, urbanization, delinquency, family dislocation; and that of initiator or facilitator of change through changes in organization, institutions, groups, resource allocation, and social relations.[2]

More knowledge and greater skill and flexibility have not meant the social worker could stint or forget the values of social work. Deepened and broadened, these values have perhaps more importance than ever to social workers of the future. Concern for all people in all countries will indeed require more skills and knowledge than most social workers have yet been able to master. Social workers have a need to understand more about alcoholism, drug abuse, child battering, of course, but they also need to know more about legislative process and the administrative process, both formal and informal. They need to know not only about blacks, Chicanos, native Americans, Puerto Ricans and their cultures, but also more about the cultures of modern European, Asian and African countries, and how these affect the United States. Sanders says:

> Special competence would have to be developed in working with ethnic minorities, and religious and cultural groups to understand their aspirations and to help develop policies that would ensure greater justice to them. Opportunity should be provided for work with ethnic groups to help understand their traditions, family patterns, cultural symbols and sex and age roles, to mention only a few.[3]

Clearly, the acquisition of such knowledge will take a lifetime. But an awareness of their shortcomings and a desire to improve themselves may well make social workers the envy of other, more scientifically oriented professionals.

---

[2] Sanders, Daniel, "Educating Change Agents for a Pluralistic Society," *Journal of the Council on Social Work Education*, vol. 10. (Spring, 1974), pp. 86–91.

[3] Ibid., p. 90.

Summary

The future of social work, like its history will be bound up with other systems and subsystems. But whatever occurs in the immediate or more remote future, social workers will need to continue to improve their knowledge and skills and to retain and expand their traditional values, even, or perhaps particularly among, the least traditional client groups.

Appendix A

The following case study describes a student project in child welfare carried on by graduate students in field placement at a state university. The students had studied various social work methods on campus and had also had course work in social policy and human behavior and research. The project demonstrates some of the ways in which theoretical information can be integrated and used in a generic setting.*

A demonstration of new methods in child welfare: A student project

Patricia C. Griffin

A project carried out by a group of graduate social work students in a facility within a mainly black, low-income area offers evidence of the effectiveness of innovative techniques, and discloses problems facing black and white staff members.

The apprenticeship model in field instruction for graduate social work students is largely a thing of the past. Because of the autonomy and flexibility of their role, students are in an excellent position for

---

* Originally printed in *Child Welfare*, vol. 52 no. 7 (July 1973). Reproduced with permission of The Child Welfare League of America.

innovation and experimentation. Ambiguity built into the student role and resultant imbalance, once thought of as disadvantages, provide an impetus toward change. The rapid shift of values and the changing life-styles occasioned by participation in the larger university community aid the student in working with client groups, which are also experiencing rapid cultural change.

Thus, a group of Florida State University students, with unprogrammed minds and unhampered by institutionalized practices in the child welfare field, have turned a haphazard social agency in the black community of Tallahassee, Florida, into a living project of substantial service to the community. Working as a team on a 4½-month block placement, they invested themselves heavily in the natural environment of a group of children and their families. Because of daily association and consequent entry into each others' behavioral orbits, the two groups—the student team (plus the volunteers who were recruited) and the clients—had considerable impact on each other. A partial acculturation began to occur on both sides, the conscious use of which provided a climate for change as the project evolved.

The project

Tallahassee, Florida, where this unit of students was based, is a medium-sized city, the capital of the state. A large part of the economic life of the town revolves around the state government and the two universities, Florida A and M and Florida State University. In Tallahassee there is a substantial middle class, a small skilled-labor group and a large unskilled labor group, mainly black. The group in the lowest economic level is centered in Frenchtown, in the geographic shadow of Florida State University.

The families in Frenchtown were experiencing spiraling stress at the time the project started. There was the depressed labor market, the perceived threat of land acquisition by the university, the further threat of a stringent enforcement of the housing code, and the other health and social problems usual in a deteriorating area. Many of the children in the community had never been outside its four square miles until, in the fall of 1970, Lincoln School, in the middle of Frenchtown, was closed and the children were sent outside to previously all-white schools. There was a lingering bitterness over the loss of the elementary school, which had served as a unifying influence. Many parents were angered because their children walked almost two miles to a school on the west side of town in a middle-class neighborhood. The community of French-town, although somewhat cohesive because of family and church, was poorly organized for problem-solving.

The graduate student group was composed of six students, two black and four white, with an equal division between men and women. The age range was from 23 to 42 years. Four had had social work experience prior to graduate school. The personalities of members of the group were markedly diverse, a factor that contributed to the experimental atmosphere and learning experience. The field instructor, who had a conventional child-welfare background, was white, female and middle-aged.

We operated through a continuing-dialogue process, formal in the Friday group meeting and informal throughout the daily routine. The field instructor's role was more enabling and consultative than didactic, reflecting a general trend in graduate field instruction, but especially pertinent to our evolving methodological focus.

The physical setup

The seat of operations was a dilapidated building called the Human Resources Clearing House. It was on a grassy corner, with another smaller house in the rear that had been used as a boys club and later was reopened for this purpose. The Clearing House, a United Fund agency, functioned haphazardly with no clear-cut program and usually without a director. It had served as a dabbling place for those who wanted to plan activities for the "underprivileged" children of Talla-hassee. White churches, sororities and fraternities arranged picnics and outings, or now and then started a group for some purpose. As a last attempt to see if this agency could function in a meaningful, planned way, the Urban League of Tallahassee was asked to coordinate the program, and the graduate student storefront field unit was asked to experiment with setting up an ongoing program.

The project's beginning was low key. One advantage was that the neighborhood children felt that the building was theirs. They were accustomed to seeing black and white people going in and out, but the presence of a new group consistently on the premises provoked curiosity. A bold few checked it out; the news raced through the grapevine and we were in business. Within 3 weeks about 50 or 60 children ranging in age from 4 to 14 were there on a daily basis.

After some observation and experimentation, groups were formed, in most instances using the nucleus of a natural group. A minimum supply of athletic and play equipment was bought and craft and school materials were scrounged from diverse places. The interior of the large building was painted on a "Paint Saturday"; the small building was patched up, and the pool table was resurfaced. This cleanup served to bond students, children and volunteers in a common enterprise at the outset. Home visits were made to the families of all of the children who came to the center regularly. The visits helped us to get acquainted, explain the program, ask for suggestions and enlist community participation.

Tutoring a major function

A tutoring program was instituted through the cooperation of the Black Student Union at Florida State. This program, initially thought of as an auxiliary service, became central to the whole operation, probably because the hostile white school environment was the point of most concern for the children and their families. Almost every child in the group needed tutoring. Conferences and group meetings were arranged between parents and teachers, between teachers and tutors. We transported parents to the schools for conferences, or went ourselves when the parent was unable to or where advocacy was indicated. Differences in role functioning in the two environments, neighborhood and school, were extreme. In general, the children were quiet, repressed, docile and even dull-appearing in school, and loud, aggressive, boisterous and noisy in the neighborhood. Clearly, such differential role functioning works to the disadvantage of the total personality. We began to think of the Clearing House operation as a kind of halfway house between home and school, with some of the unstructured elements of the former and the structured elements of the latter.

The student task force, working flexibly as a problem-solving medium, began to develop helping modes, a few innovative, others a combination of established, even old-fashioned techniques or methods.

The agency as a therapeutic milieu

The environment of the house began to emerge as a therapeutic one, promoting individual and group development. The center almost became an extended family for many of the children. Since most of the parents either worked or were caring for large families, the children had been roving the neighborhood in loose-knit groups. There was a wide age range in these groups because many of the girls had responsibility for younger siblings. After the facility was in full swing, many children came there directly from school, with their parents' knowledge and permission.

Each afternoon there was a checkup in the office of notes from teachers or homework to be done. (A student-in-charge carried on this role.) Children kept after school telephoned in for rides home. One day a whole group rushed in waving notices about the children's symphony, with requests, "Can we go? Please can we go?" Arrangements were made to take the group.

We believed that to be effective we could not deviate too far from the familiar cultural patterns of the children. To anyone entering the house for the first time it appeared chaotic; the noise was deafening at times. This bothered us at first, but gradually the situation began to seem normal, and the basic threads within the confusion were easier to discern. Nonverbal communication no longer seemed a quirk of the black poverty group, or evidence of backwardness. At times it was the only functional method of communication. The students began to fall into the same communication patterns, using a look or a touch for imparting important messages and word play as part of informal interaction.

Out of the association of children, students, tutors and volunteers, group norms emerged; helping elements were utilized as they surfaced; formal and informal sanctions were formulated. The rules were simple: "No one breaks into a club meeting," "No cussing," "No fighting in the house," "No one tears up what someone else is doing," "No one brings food into the house unless he has enough to share."

We kept a daily record of occurrences in the house for ongoing evaluation purposes. Dysfunctional trends could be spotted before they became problems; positive trends could be accelerated or combined.

Casework and group work

In the feedback meetings we identified problems common to the whole group and those representing individual malfunctioning. The better adjusted children (perhaps those with more social skills) related equally well with all members of the staff. A child with problems formed an intense relationship with only one or sometimes two adults. The assumption was that such selectivity was probably based on unconscious factors, representing a problem-solving thrust on the part of the child. By common professional consent, the child's choice became his worker. If a child formed a meaningful association with a volunteer, that person was aided in helping the child. As a child worked through problem levels, he often changed to another helper. A small boy who had lacked mothering all his life first picked out a middle-aged woman student, but as his needs became less poignant, he progressed to a positive association with the young man who was his club leader.

As a group the staff were aware of the individual prescription agreed upon for each child, so that any staff member could work with the child to cope with any problems that arose. For example, firmness was the order for Charlene; James needed small, informal group activities so that he could make the transition into one of the boys clubs; Anna May's wails were to be treated casually, so as not to reinforce the baby role assigned to her by family and neighborhood.

An attempt was made to help dysfunctional pairs, in addition to working with individual children. Two nine-year-old girls who were openly engaging together in erotic caressing and two little boys who were acting out together, one the planner, the other the doer, were pairs that presented a challenge. In these instances, as in others, the group experience and individual counseling (formal and informal) were used as interlocking elements in the treatment plan.

Staff members became accustomed to on-the-spot casework, plugging in when and where needed—on the premises, in the homes, at school. Knowing the positive coping mechanisms of the children and their families, we were in a more strategic helping position than a worker seeing the family for the first time in a situation of stress. A problem often could be identified and remedied before it reached major proportions. Assistance could be provided casually. When it was necessary for a family to mobilize itself to seek aid of a regular social agency, we acted as a referral source.

New adaptations

The project's largest concern was helping its whole client group and their families to learn skills effective in meeting the social pressures applied by the larger community. Such things as promoting rapprochement between the schools and the community, decreasing fears and misunderstandings, and demonstrating to the children and their parents methods of advocating for themselves, were some of the goals.

We enlisted whatever parent participation we could. A father who was a sign painter made a new sign, mothers helped in group activities, and older siblings were effective assistant leaders.

Through informal role model demonstration, some of the older siblings learned better ways of nurturing young children. Since girls in the black poverty culture carry heavy responsibility for younger children in their families, this seemed an effective family entry point. As older siblings watched the tutors, they learned how to help with homework.

The emphasis with all of the children was on self-help, on development of positive self-images and leadership skills, on building on the positive elements of their own culture as a baseline resource for trying new coping mechanisms and for solving problems.

Problems

The student group encountered many problems. After the project had been in full swing for several months, a family group of three children threatened to disrupt the whole program by their daily destructive activities. While were were considering telling their mother that the children could not attend anymore, a curious thing happened. The atmosphere of the house began to change their behavior, rather than the reverse. The setting evidently functioned much like that of a corrective part-time foster home. This was convincing evidence that we had created a healthy environment capable of incorporating negative input.

Problems developed within the student group. There was a thread of black-white confrontation that threatened at several points to dissolve the team approach. The blacks charged the whites with being overly lenient in discipline, and in general with being overly sentimental. The tender approach used by some of the white students was countered by the black attitude of "It's tough out there and you better be ready for it." The blacks opposed getting too far away from the child-rearing patterns of the community, contending that doing so would downgrade significant adults in the children's lives, thus setting up another discordancy. These staff problems were compounded by the "battle fatigue" noted by Bowles as built into the white worker-black child experience.[1]

The matter of race was most often invoked when a child was upset over something else. The child was, however, as likely to deprecate a black student's blackness as a white student's whiteness, depending on the focus of his anger. We solved staff differences on racial issues through continual confrontation, discussion and compromise.

Acculturation, although part of the problem-solving medium, also had its pitfalls. The less distance some students felt from the clients and their culture, the more the students fell into some clients' feelings of hopelessness and despondency. Staff began to take on some of the group's paranoia toward the hostile white school environment. Some staff whites confided that they had moments of "thinking black."

Because of the intensity of the field experience, each student underwent a more exacting personal and professional reexamination than usually occurs in a conventional agency, where emphasis is on adaptation to a stable program. Not rocking the boat is far different from building the boat while standing in the water.

In this project it was obvious that how one came across as a person was first, and how one came across as a social worker or a black or white person was second. Concealing inappropriate personal components behind a professional mien was ruled out. Flexibility was essential to work in the joint task.

Results and implications for practice

Within four to six weeks after the project started, there was some positive feedback from families and schools. These comments centered

---

[1] Bowles, Dorcas D., "Making Casework Relevant to Black People: Approaches, Techniques, Theoretical Implications," *Child Welfare*, 48, 8 (Oct. 1969), pp. 468–74.

around enhanced school and social functioning and reinforced staff observations of improvement in self-image and interactional skills of many of the children. Equally observable were attitudinal shifts and skill development in the student team and in some of the volunteers.

A report of the project was filed with the board of directors of the Clearing House and with the United Fund. Two of the students also wrote a consultant's report as part of an advanced practice course. Subsequently, the United Fund increased the funding base of the Clearing House, a federal grant was made, and a paid professional director was hired. The program continues on a sound basis.

The results support the thesis that child welfare services must be moved to the children and their families where they are—geographically, culturally, and emotionally. "Starting where the client is" should not refer only to his emotional life space. Further, this old professional adage implies the converse proposition of starting where the worker is—culturally as well as professionally. If we are learning anything from work based in poverty neighborhoods, it is understanding the impact of the helped on the helper and on the helping process.

We have been restricted by service function modalities, mostly remedial, that often function to perpetuate cultural maladaptations or even to foster new ones. The child welfare worker must begin to think of himself in a larger context, assuming a mediating role for children on the intrapsychic, interpersonal, intrafamilial, intraneighborhood and intercultural levels. Projects such as the one described could be equally applicable with children in, say, a suburban middle-class area where alienation is creating individual and community problems. Results possible from such conscious use of a social work team vis-à-vis a client group are open-ended. Exposure of graduate students to this kind of experimentation enriches their learning experience, as well as contributing to methodological innovation in the social work discipline.

Questions

THE PROJECT

1. What systems seem to be involved in the project (chap. 2)?
2. How many kinds of communities are described (chap. 7)?
3. If you were to start a community organization project in the Tallahassee community, what kinds of information about the community would you need (chap. 7)?
4. What is the difference between a community and a system (chap. 2)?

THE PHYSICAL SETUP

1. Explain the reference to "graduate student storefront field unit."
2. Do you think this term refers to a system or a community (chaps. 2 and 7)?
3. What do you think of the setting for the project, personally and professionally?
4. Would you, as a student social worker, feel comfortable working in that setting? Why (chaps. 1 and 4)?
5. Which of the stages of planned change do you see described in the first two sections of the article (chap. 2)?
6. Of the initiations of the planned change process listed in chapter 4, which do you think are most likely in this project?
7. What methods of social work can you identify in this project? Which worker roles?
8. What factors of group composition are identified (chap. 5)?

TUTORING

1. What is your reaction to the term "hostile" white school environment?
2. What does the word "role" mean when it is applied to the children at the center? How do the children perceive their roles?
3. Can you visualize the social worker in the role of tutor? What other roles are played by the student social workers in the tutoring process?

THE AGENCY AS A THERAPEUTIC MILIEU

1. What is meant by "therapeutic milieu"?
2. Which of Schwartz's central tasks do you see described in this section (chap. 4)?
3. What kinds of knowledge were the student social workers expected to have and to use?
4. What kinds of knowledge did the clients (the children) have to share with the student workers?
5. How does the concept of symbiosis apply here?

CASEWORK AND GROUP WORK

1. Can you think of some problems which might be identified in feedback meetings?
2. Can you structure an interview using some ideas from this section?
3. What knowledge of human behavior would be needed by a student worker?
4. Give some examples of intervention with individuals, with families, or with groups which might come about as a result of feedback meetings.
5. Do you think the groups described are task or growth groups? Give examples.

6. What instances do you see of a student social worker acting as a mediator?
7. Give some examples of long-range and short-range goals sought by workers and children.
8. Can you see any examples of maintenance or stabilization of change?

PROBLEMS

1. How do the problems in this section differ from those in the preceding sections?
2. What implications do you see for racial confrontation between workers or between workers and clients?
3. What kinds of knowledge would the student workers need to have about themselves?
4. What do you think is the meaning of "start where the client is"?
5. Do you see this project as a kind of prevention? Explain.
6. Do you think undergraduate students could function in this project?
7. Describe a project which you would like to work with. What methods, what roles, what systems would be involved?

Appendix B

The "Twelfth of May" is a real-life account of a project in community work. Like most such projects, it is vitally and closely associated with a variety of individual, group and community systems. The interview was taped in March, 1966, and is reproduced here from an uncorrected copy of a transcript that was circulating in 1973.*

The Twelfth of May

An interview with Paul Kurzman, Staff Associate of the Two Bridges Neighborhood Council. Paul staffed the Program Planning Committee for the Two Bridges Summer Reading Program, a neighborhood community action project.

Question
Paul, will you introduce yourself a bit and discuss your role, as you came in on the planning for the Two Bridges program.

---

* Printed with permission of the author, Paul A. Kurzman. Paul A. Kurzman has served as Staff Director of the Two Bridges Neighborhood Council and as Acting Executive Director of the Lower Eastside Neighborhoods Association (LENA) in New York City. He was Assistant Commissioner of the Youth Services Agency in New York's Human Resources Administration, and Director of New York City's $30 million-a-year Neighborhood Youth Corps program. He has served as a social welfare consultant in both the public and private sectors, is editor of a book on social welfare practices, *The Mississippi Experience: Strategies for Welfare Rights Action*, and author of *Harry Hopkins and the New Deal*. Dr. Kurzman is Assistant Professor, Hunter College School of Social Work, City University of New York.

Answer

Well, I am a social worker, trained as a community organizer, and my role is as staff worker of the Two Bridges Neighborhood Council, assigned and paid by LENA, the Lower Eastside Neighborhoods Association, to do community work in the area between the Brooklyn and Manhattan Bridges on New York's Lower Eastside, specifically with the Two Bridges Neighborhood Council, a LENA affiliate.

What I wanted to talk about today is what I was able to see from the vantage point of my role in the Summer Reading Program. I staffed the program planning committee, and along with the lay chairman of the committee, the lay chairman of the Council, and the committee members, was responsible for much of the routine administration of the program before it actually took place on the 6th of July.

Let me begin by saying a little bit about the Council. The Council is composed of lay and professional people who live in the area in and around the entrance to the Manhattan and Brooklyn Bridges on the Lower Eastside of Manhattan.

It has been going for ten years, that is, since 1955, when it began interestingly enough, out of interest which lay community people had in remedial reading. They felt there was a real need to have remedial reading programs in the community to supplement the programs which their children were receiving in school.

And the really momentous and interesting aspect is that on the 10th Anniversary of the Neighborhood Council, it has really come full cycle from the initial germ, by which it began, which is remedial reading, with a very minute program within Hamilton-Madison Settlement House and some of the local churches, to a program financed by the Government for $105,000 for 40 youngsters. The Council itself operates out of a fairly modest store front on Madison Street, which is a converted two-chair barbershop.

Let me, then, tell you what took place between 1955, when the Council started, and 1964, when the real activity began on planning this year's program.

Attempts were made in the past by Margaret Z. of Mariners' Temple and by my predecessor as staff associate, to get programs in remedial reading sponsored by the Board of Education. They met with very little success, because, as I understand it, it was the feeling of the Assistant Superintendent in the area that such a program could not possibly be successful because the parents were not really interested in the education of their children, and that they would never have their children come to any large-scale program, even if you went to the trouble of organizing it.

In spite of these rebuffs, in the summer of 1964, the Two Bridges Neighborhood Council did sponsor a modest summer reading program for approximately 100 neighborhood children. It was funded at the last minute, in late May or early June, with Mobilization For Youth Funds, and at the time of funding rapid organization was done to try to get a program underway and really an amazingly good job was done with the last-minute notice and the few thousand ($3,000 or $4,000) that was made available to the community.

We had no research components in the program, and there was no community coordinator, no teacher or volunteer trainer, very little lay involvement, very little feedback, and very little of what is today called "infection" of the program among the lay people in the Two Bridges community. So that while it was successful in helping youngsters improve their reading capacity over the summer, last year's—the 1964 program—really did not embody those significant community organization components that would make it much more than remedial reading alone.

Although the community was aware of this, they could do very little about it, because they did not either have the time or the money to do more than they had done. After the summer of 1964 there was a feeling that these programs were important and should be continued after school, during the regular school year. And with Mobilization For Youth and other monies, homework help programs were continued on an after-school basis in local public schools, settlements and churches.

The nature of the programs were so wide and so diverse that the Two Bridges Area Youth Team's Case Clearance Committee (an organization of neighborhood professionals) took it as a task to try to coordinate the various after-school homework help programs, which they did, and they published a guide.

This bit of background will give you a little idea of the long-term standing interest in remedial reading and community development that have been in the Two Bridges community (somewhat latent) waiting for the money, the time, and the organizational capacities to harness a summer reading program of the size, scope, and meaning of the one held in the summer of 1965.

Now, let me tell you what went into the 1965 program. On October 6, 1964, the Acting Assistant Superintendent of the Board of Education,

Districts 1–4, called together interested persons in the Two Bridges community, LENA and Mobilization For Youth to meet in his office to evaluate last year's program for 100 youngsters and, if appropriate, to plan a bigger program for the coming 1965 summer.

It was well attended, and from this meeting a committee was appointed by the Assistant Superintendent, with the consent of the Council, to go about developing a program proposal for 1965, and to carry it through to the point of judging and hiring of staff. It had, therefore, for the first time in the history of the Two Bridges community of which I'm aware, the formal blessing of the Board of Education, which is extremely significant.

Question
Paul, before you go any further, I'd like to stop for a minute here, and try to isolate what we took into the meeting in the Assistant Superintendent's office in October, what we were able to isolate that had made the 1964 program successful, and what the nature of that meeting was, in terms of people lined up either for or more or less against a new program of this kind of scope.

Answer
I wouldn't want to oversimplify the nature of this program, and make it seem all honey and cream. It was not. There was still a strong resistance on the part of some educational officials, and I think it would be fair to say, some resistance on the part of the Acting Superintendent, to developing a program. But the experience and the success of the past summer, the enthusiasm of the parents and the eagerness of the professional staff and the lay leaders of the Two Bridges Neighborhood Council began to snowball and I think that the Assistant Superintendent saw at the beginning of that meeting that the cards were on the table, and like it or not, with or without his blessing, the community was going to go ahead. He probably felt that there would be more for him to gain by being on our side than by trying to fight us, because the 1964 summer had proven that the previous Assistant Superintendent was dead wrong, that parents are interested; they will bring their children; the children will enjoy it; and most important, they will learn something.

Having had his predecessor proven wrong, I think how he felt—this was a bandwagon and he'd better tie himself to a good thing rather than be on the records as opposed to it. Also, within that meeting, there were strong factions and these factions we should be aware of. On the one hand there were a group of people there who were not eager to have this program expanded, and certainly not eager to have it expanded privately, that is by a neighborhood council, outside of the control of the

Board of Education.

That group was pitted against another group that was absolutely determined to have the program and equally determined to make sure it was outside of the auspices of the Board of Education (but, if feasible, with their blessing). If not possible, in spite of their blessing!

Question
Can you discuss, then, Paul, some of the factors which our 1964 program administrator isolated that were strengths and weaknesses of the 1964 program; and can you also give a flavor of the support which noneducational professional people in the community offered him at that meeting?

Answer
Yes, I think that our administrator isolated the potential strengths of the children; that these were *not* stupid children, as they had been called for so long by so many people; that they were, in fact, bright children who showed an incredible ability just to cope with life under adverse conditions; and that with appropriate attention that they could learn in an environment where things were individualized and adapted to the youngster's own particular needs. Therefore, the children were excited, and he knew they were excited. The parents were excited and he knew they were excited, too.

As for the teachers, we only had a couple of teachers in the 1964 program and a few assistant teachers on a volunteer basis. They were, in the most part, public school teachers, who, as I understand it, were quite different in the summer reading program than they were in the usual school year. With the freedom of not having to clock in and out, not being checked up on, and not having the bureaucratic restraints that a large system such as the Board of Education puts on people, they, in fact, came out with the spontaneity, the initiative, the affection, and the brightness within them that actually made the program a success.

An interesting learning which came out of the 1964 program which the Administrator was able to spell out in this meeting led us to a way of selecting teachers for the second program. One of the teachers came in without sufficient background and knowledge of a community such as ours to be able to move to solving children's learning problems. She was still so shocked and taken aback by the nature of the experiences the children brought into her classroom that she stayed in shock for several weeks, not able to attend to reading problems. Other teachers, because they came out of a neighborhood similar to the children, were immediately able, without pause and shock and falling back, to attend to reading problems; and the Administrator was able to see, even in that small program, that to get teachers for the second summer he was going to have to do very careful screening and attempt to get teachers who had already become aware of, both emotionally and intellectually, the problems that children and families such as these bring in to a program of the kind we were to plan this summer.

In answer to the second part of your question, the key to the fact that this program came off (and the key in that meeting in the Assistant Superintendent's office), was that there was a fair balance of power between educational people pro and against having a larger summer reading program; with this balance, the people that carried it were the lay and the professional people in the Two Bridges community. The lay people who lead the Two Bridges Neighborhood Council, and the professional people (social workers, educators and ministers) came into that meeting *absolutely determined* that they were going to have a summer reading program, and there wasn't a thing in the world, not the least of which was the Board of Education, who could possibly stop them. They hoped for the Board of Education's blessing, but they made it expressly clear to themselves and expressly clear in the meeting that with or without the Board of Education this program was going to take place; this was the key factor which I think every community who wants to develop a similar program should remember: that even if you can't get the approval of the city and Board of Education sources, that if your lay and professional people in the community want it deep enough, they are more influential than any elected or appointed official in the City.

Question
Paul, let's try to summarize, when you speak of lay people in the meeting, the kind of lay person you mean. I want us not to give an impression that we took in with us 100 indigenous leaders. I want to talk about what the lay leadership in this Council is, and what implications that had for the success of this program.

Answer
The lay people we had there were people like the chairman of our Council, a person who has lived here all his life, not a person with a college education, but a person who knows the community, is deeply committed to the people that live here, and who has about ten years of on-the-spot experience of dealing with city officials under his belt; people like the cochairman of the Education Committee, who has experience in running an Education Committee, a Parent Association, and deep involvement in many other agencies and community organizations within the Two Bridges area. These people are, in many ways, more sophisticated than many of the pros. They know the ropes, and

they know what their community needs much better than professionals who might have only been here one or two years. They were born here; they have often lived all their life here; and their parents lived all their lives here before them. They know what their children need, and they have a commitment which no money would buy, a commitment which only their life's involvement in living here could bring.

Then, for other communities trying to bring about programs such as these, some will not have visible people like these already working in the community, as we were fortunate to have; that is, lay people with this kind of background, commitment, and length of service. For many communities there will be an even bigger job than we had of finding lay leadership.

This leads to a very important point: that this program did not develop out of a mass community interest. This was not a program where hundreds of laymen knocked on the doors of the Board of Education and said, "We want it." This program, for good or for bad, was planned, organized and achieved by a fairly small group of active laymen who were leaders of the Two Bridges Neighborhood Council, plus a group of progressive, enlightened professional people whom the community is most fortunate to have. This is planned by more people, by more of the parents of the youngsters who were in the program, more of the "indigenous poor," but the point of fact is that it wasn't planned by these people. As near as we got were the lay leaders of the Council, and that is certainly not identical to the "indigenous poor." Next year we very much plan to have more parents of the youngsters in the program on the program-planning committee. They will develop the next program. But we were not ready, at this stage; the opposition was still so great, that many felt it would probably take the sophistication and experience of certain lay leaders and certain professionals to accomplish the task in 1965. I have mixed feelings here, but in 1966, things are going to be quite different, and already steps are underway to assure that it will be.

The only time that a real mass expression come forth was at the time of our picketing, and later in our discussion we will come to that, because of its tremendous significance in terms of community organization, and what lay people can do to make a city buckle under.

Now, let's go to what happened after that meeting at the Assistant Superintendent's office when the Superintendent set up a committee charged with planning the program for 1965.

There was a strong disagreement as to who was to chair this committee and under whose auspices the committee was to be. It was the feeling of some education people that it was to be chaired by a Principal in the neighborhood and to be run generally under Board of Ed. aegis; and it was the feeling of another group of people that it was to be chaired by the co-chairman of the Education Committee of the Two Bridges Neighborhood Council, and run under the Two Bridges Neighborhood Council and a community aegis.

This became a point of clear and sharp disagreement. I, as the worker, was centrally involved in this conflict, and it was a really sharp one. The Council took a position which I was charged to express to the Principal on their behalf: that we would not stand for anything less than sponsorship of this program by the Neighborhood Council and by the lay people in the community; that it would be chaired by a lay person, that meetings would be held at the Council office; but that no appropriate body in the community would be excluded, least of all officials of the Board of Education. We took an absolutely firm stand with the Acting Assistant Superintendent on it, and won.

From this point, we held meetings about every two or three weeks, at the Neighborhood Council office, called by the chairman or the Program Planning Committee. They were the most active, productive meetings of their kind that I can remember in my brief experience in the field. We began with a topical agenda composed by the Planning Committee Chairman Mr. K. (who administered last year's program), the chairman of our Council, and myself. Then we sat down at session after session, and filled out the agenda, under sections stating what should teacher training and volunteer hiring be like; when should the program hours be; what type of research component should be; should we have community coordinators or should we not; would there be books for youngsters; if so, what type of books should we use; who should administer the program; what type of staff and staff accountability should there be; what type of budgets would be necessary to finance a program of the size and scope that we wanted; what type of lay citizen involvement should there be; what kind of balance should there be between public and parochial children; on and on.

I would say there were about 15 of these meetings. After each meeting, what we had discussed in the meeting I wrote up, and sent around in draft form to everyone who attended. Then, when we came back to the next meeting, they could discuss their objections to the drafts, and after changes were made, this progress was incorporated into the final draft, which was to become the proposal.

As one can see from the proposal, it was decided that many new innovations were to brought into this program that were not present last year.

That the program would be expanded from 120 children, initially (I em-phasize initially) to perhaps 200 children. That one community coordi-nator and a part-time teacher-trainer were to be included; that the cost of the program was to be expanded from $3,000 or $4,000 to $20,000; from a program without parent involvement to parent involvement through trilingual parent workshops; a program to include a Higher Horizons Program on Friday for the youngsters; to include building home libraries through free paperbacks to be given to youngsters to take home each week; to use some of the newest books in remedial reading including the Bank Street series, the Skyline, Scott-Foresman and SRA. There was no formal research component, or no clinic in-cluded in the original thinking.

Finally, after months and months of work—I would say, well over 100 hours just spent in meetings alone, and at least another 100 to 200 hours of my own time as staff worker writing up what came out of the meetings, getting them into minutes, rewriting the minutes, and finally, out of all the minutes combined—came a proposal. This initial modest 7-page proposal for $20,000 was developed around Christmas Time and by early January we now in our committee meetings turned to the important question of funding.

The natural question is: There were so many hours involved, when was all this planning done? The people on the Program Planning Com-mittee—didn't they have anything anything else to do in life? If so, when could they possibly find what I would estimate to be at least the 200 hours that were required? The answer: it was done on their own time.

The lay people like Mrs. D., a housewife with three children, were not and to this date have never been financially compensated in any way for all of the hours which they put into planning the program. They were done on hours when she would get babysitters to take care of her chil-dren; they were done sometimes at night, after she had given her hus-band dinner, and she would stay up late and write drafts; they were done by people like Harry L., our Council chairman, who would take time off from work without pay to be at meetings; he would come in at night when he had to work days, and review drafts, and leave his notes for me to incorporate the next day. There were people like Pam C., and Margaret Z., who were neighborhood education and social service workers, to meet with us and to work on their own together on Satur-days, Sundays, and late hours at night. There were people like Dick K., who is an Assistant Principal, who after 3:00 o'clock, when he was no longer responsible for school program, would give of his own hours here, from 3:00 to 5:00, and then go home and work again at night, once again on his own. Myself, I am a social worker, and one of my responsibilities is to staff this council. I work a 35-hour week. I am paid for a 35-hour week. I averaged a 70-hour week last year. I spend as much time as my wife permits.

When it came now to funding, we were determined not to go to the Board of Education for very good reasons. If they were to fund it, they would have every right to control it, and the committee did not want this. The Board of Education people on the committee frankly did not want it anymore than did the non-Board people. We both realized the large limitations that would be placed on us if the Board held the purse strings. We're at January. The big thing we were lacking now was *money*. In our meetings, we all divided up responsibility for approaching different service and other church council groups in the City as well as their own denominations; a member of the committee who was on the executive committee of Mobilization For Youth was going to join the Council in an approach to Mobilization. A member of the committee who knew certain influential people in foundations in the City was going to use his influence with these foundations. On and on. This was the "shotgun approach."

It ended up this way. We sent out letters to 15 foundations. Good letters, incorporating the report of our last year's program, our proposal for this year's program, and a pretty good defense of why we should be funded. We approached Mobilization, and had individual negotiations with them. And the church contacts were also explored. The long and short of it is, we "struck out" in most every area. Mobilization for Youth indicated that they did not see where they would be able (in their World of Education program) to give a sum as large as $20,000 to one program in the Two Bridges area. But said that they may—reserving many promises until later—be able to give a very small amount of money to sponsor certain aspects of the program, but could give us no pledge until well into spring.

All 15 foundations that we approached by general mailing gave us negative answers. The two foundations which one of the clergymen approached did come through with small grants. One made a grant of $3,500, and the other a grant of $500. So, we at least had $4,000 which we regarded as seed money.

This, of course, excited the committee. The hopelessness of coming back every week and hearing "no, no, no," all this work you've gone to, the wonderful program that you feel you've set up, and no one wants to fund you. There were fits of great depression during those weeks. Hopelessness. Feelings of what does it mean if a committee goes to all this trouble and the neighborhood sponsors a program, and all of the foundations and people who have money are not going to support it; if they won't support us, who in the heck are they going to support?

Well, then came the brilliant turn, the turn that was the key to all of the funding for this program in 1965. About this time (late January) the expansion of the federal Anti-Poverty Program was getting in the press, and becoming something that might now filter down into local communities. A major decision was made at a meeting in late January that we would now approach the City's Anti-Poverty Board and the Office of Economic Opportunity to have our program financed with OEO funds. On the 16th of March a delegation from the committee of Mrs. D., Mr. L., Margaret Z., myself and two others met with the Educational Specialist of the New York City Anti-Poverty Board staff and presented our proposal. The proposal met with great enthusiasm by the two staff workers in charge of reviewing all education proposals for the City. They felt it was an extraordinary proposal, in keeping with all of the requirements of Anti-Poverty funding, and the only suggestion they had was for its expansion.

Question

Paul, as an educational consultant to your committee, I was with you that day, and it occurs to me that the first response we got there was that the best thing we could do for the program was to turn it into a pre-kindergarten program. I think you ought to talk a little about this strength that you had with you, in the professional people who had a knowledge of the research that was going on, and who could also help back up the reasons for carrying through our goals.

Answer

This is an important aspect. I think with my being a professional, my own bias is to give all the credit to lay people, but I think it was the unique blend of experienced and committed lay people with the most talented group of professionals I've seen anywhere that made the difference—a group of professionals who had skills everywhere from the experts in remedial reading for elementary school youngsters to people experienced in community development, parent participation, and the homely but necessary art of proposal preparation.

Together all of these people formed a team. People got along so well together. They respected each other's abilities. The laymen respected the professional for his talents, and the professional the laymen for what only the laymen could do. This was a key ingredient.

You are absolutely right. They wanted to make this into a "Head Start." We simply said we do not have Head Start in mind, and when we were firm and clear enough, they finally backed down.

The New York City Anti-Poverty Board did want it substantially expanded, and we were happy to do so. Among the things they wanted included were a research component, more community coordinators, a full-time teacher-trainer, a clinic library, a process film and eyeglasses for youngsters: and the amazing thing they did was to tell us on the 16th of March that they wanted this all incorporated, the proposal completely redrafted and a hundred copies on their desk no later than a week from that date.

The committee, by now, was used to almost anything. I, as the worker who had prepared the first proposal draft, was charged by the committee (after it had met again and outlined the way they wanted it done) with rewriting the proposal and rebudgeting it, and submitting a draft back to the committee for approval.

I have a number of other responsibilities to the Council, to include staffing its Housing and Planning Division, sports committees, 8-page newspaper, area youth team, executive committee, and health committee, etc. With the approval of my Council chairman, I cancelled out of every meeting which I had been lined up to go to for the next week, cancelled my supervisory conferences with my own supervisee, and my supervisory conferences with my own supervisor, cancelled my weekend plans and literally devoted one week, night and day, to nothing else but this proposal.

It might look easy, but we were required to get three quotes for every item we were going to rent or buy for the summer. That means we had to make telephone calls for every tape recorder, for every SRA book, for every Skyline series, for every typewriter, for every fan, to three people in New York City to get the lowest bids.

It was an amazing process. Each person took on their own share. People like Pam and Margaret and Harry M. took on the responsibility for getting all the quotes on the books. And this was beautiful. In they came with the library requisition lists, and all the material which I would incorporate in the final draft.

My secretary and two of the laymen took on a lot of the responsibility for calling up Peerless and Willoughbys and stores like that for the other rentals. I did calls to the Community Council and all over the City to try to come up with parity salaries, so that ours would be equitable. Calls and letters went out to try to find out how much glasses would cost, how much it would cost to get optometrists. Margaret Z., with friends of hers, found out how much it would cost to do the films, and came up with a detailed budget breakdown for two ten-minute runs. It was the most extraordinary week that I can remember! It was a week in which people saw that there was a funding source in sight. This kept us going.

By the end of the week, we had a draft of the proposal. We also decided that it would be exceptionally important to have letters of support from all neighborhood organizations, and if possible, from the Board of Education. Each member of the committee took responsibility for getting letters from their organization and from allied ones. I took responsibility for negotiatiing with the Board of Education to see if we could get a letter from Dr. Donovan. I also took responsibility for requesting support from Mobilization For Youth.

Through an example of what would be technically called cooperation, we involved the Livingston Street Board of Education to a degree where they were actually delighted to give us a letter, signed by Dr. Donovan, the head of the school system in the City of New York, supporting the Two Bridges Neighborhood Council's program, to which, for five to ten years previously, their own Assistant Superintendent had been adamantly opposed. I cannot underestimate the importance of this letter, because Dr. Donovan is one of the people that sat on the City committee which had to approve this proposal, two weeks later; and naturally everyone on the committee, when an education proposal comes before them, turns to Donovan, and says, "Do you bless this, or do you not?" When they saw his own letter with the proposal, they didn't even bother to turn to him. He didn't even need to be at the meeting. They knew that we had the Board of Education support. We had support of the Catholic churches, the Protestant churches, LENA, Mobilization For Youth and all of these letters accompanied our proposal to the City.

Meantime, we were negotiating with the federal regional OEO representative, a wonderful person, to insure that there would be federal support if this got through the City. He was able to give us a tentative commitment.

Meanwhile, we were contacting all of our elected representatives. This was another important community organization factor. Our own congressman, Leonard Farbstein, wrote 14 letters on our behalf, to OEO, to the City—to all the important people who needed to be contacted—indicating that he, as our representative, was behind us. We got our city councilman and our two senators, Javits and Kennedy, behind us. It got to a point where it was so obvious that we were going to get support from every element of the community, that in the words of the chairman of our committee, nobody could stop us now. Or at least they better not try.

Question

Paul, at this point while you were seeing all of the organization and people moving to support you, it was also obvious that people in the neighborhood were aware that this was happening, and that, for example, when Margaret and I would go into the hardware store after working in the church all afternoon, he would say, "Are you going to get the money, are you going to get the money?" This thing very rapidly permeated the community.

Answer

Yes. I don't want to minimize this. My tendency perhaps is to minimize this element because the support and the involvement of the community was not as large as any of us would have wanted it to be—OEO and the City say that this ought to be planned by the local indigenous people. All I can say is that was the most complex proposal I've ever written (and I had written previous proposals for government), and God help the lay indigenous people who are supposed to fill out those forms, and write proposals with the right jargon to their specifications. But we did have many people behind us, many of the mothers.

First of all, we made sure that every mother of a child in *last* year's program knew exactly what we were doing for *this* year. We used the tenant's associations, the *Two Bridges News* (which is circulated to everyone, for example, in Smith Houses, Rutgers Houses, and Knickerbocker Village) as a key channel of communication. The priests and ministers were speaking about it from their pulpits on Sunday; the Mother Superiors were speaking about it in their PTA meetings; the local schools were speaking about it in their parent associations; the local school board was talking it up at each meeting. So it was getting to be pretty well known.

Now, I move to the actual submission of the proposal to the City on the 31st of March. In other words, from the day when we first met with the City, to the day we submitted it, only 15 days had elapsed. This new, "revised" proposal was vastly different from the one before. It was now . . . not a 7-page proposal, but a proposal of 19 pages; a proposal that at least doubled the staff, doubled the "comprehensiveness," and doubled the number of children to be served. Now we were planning for 400 children plus a clinic for 50 more. It went into the City, formally submitted in 50 copies, with all the forms and accompanying letters of support, on the 31st of March with promises that we would hear from the City within a week or two, as they began putting it through their administrative structure.

Let me give you a little idea what this structure is. It had to go through two Anti-Poverty Boards in the City. The names keep changing, but briefly, one was a hierarchical committee of people appointed by the Mayor that would include, for example, the head of the Board of Education, other commissioners, and people of that bigwig level in the City. The other committee was supposed to be of professionals in the field of education, social services, health, etc., who were to examine for technical merits, whereas the bigshot committee would examine for its appropriateness in a government framework.

We waited, and we waited. We made calls to the City which went unanswered. We couldn't get through to the people we had spoken to. Our messages were never answered. Our letters were never responded to. We even pulled strings. People we knew who knew people. Contacts which some of the laymen and professionals had. We got absolutely nowhere.

The word filtered back to several of us, informally (and these are the things you never can prove), but the word was pretty reliable, that our proposal was in a way ironically "too good." What do I mean? I mean too independent. It was just too much out of the hands of central city control. It might rally the people to independently speak out against city forces (i.e., the Board of Education), which would make too many people feel uncomfortable, especially in an election year!

After six weeks, the committee met again and made a decision to send personal telegrams to the Mayor, Mr. Screvane (head of the Anti-Poverty Council), and Mrs. Roberts, the Staff Director. These telegrams were sent on the 3rd of May, briefly summarizing our grievance, the unreplied-to phone calls, the six-week delay—the complete disregard, the utter callousness with which we as a community organization were being handled, after they had told us that our proposal was good, and to submit it.

In our final sentence, we said—and this was the key that I want to emphasize what we said, and the uniqueness of our wording—"unless we hear from you within the next week, this neighborhood council will be forced to resort to measures of publicity and public protest." I say again, "publicity and public protest." Seven days later, on the 10th of May we met again. Everyone agreed that absolutely no word had been heard, writter or verbal, from anyone in the City in reply to our urgent telegrams. Our telephone calls were still ignored; we were still dirt. We were therefore fully intending to go through with our measures of publicity and public protest.

Our decision now was to determine which types of publicity and public protest would be effective and, at the same time, responsible. It was the decision of the committee, with the sanction of the executive committee of the Two Bridges Neighborhood Council (called into emergency session) that we should make our specific grievances known in a fact sheet to all newspapers, radio and television stations. We should also plan to picket the Anti-Poverty Board as our last resort, on the 12th of May.

I want to underline the sort of stages we went through. If you want to call us, going through "mania" and "depression," we were in depression back in October, when we thought the Board of Ed. was going to try to take it over; mania in November when we saw that we were going to be able to be independent; depression again in January when we couldn't get funding; mania in March when we saw we might get Anti-Poverty money, and now back into incredible depression, in April and early May.

Here we were. We had done everything they had told us to do. We had broken our backs getting the proposal in at tremendously short notice. We had rallied the support and understanding of lay and professional people in the community.

Everybody would call out when I walked into a store or walked down the street, "Hey Paul, how's it coming? Where is it? You submitted it on the 31st of March. What's happening? Is my kid going to get remedial reading this summer? Am I going to have a job? What about my children?" And all the time we had to say, "Sorry, we just don't know."

When this begins to happen—this kind of delay, this ignoring of community people and of a community organization—it feeds directly into the latent cynicism in people because they really don't think anything can be accomplished to wipe out poverty. In this month, in this span of time, that cynicism was hardened.

Then long night sessions were spent—I remember one night in which George Y. and myself and Margaret Z. were up until all hours—I don't think we ever went to bed, preparing press releases for the picketing, preparing flyer handouts for people on the street, going through the incredible organizational process of trying to inform all of the supporting bodies of what we were doing, and why we were doing it; sending letters to executive committees and to all the people in the community, telling them what we were doing, and why we were doing it. And by the way, we included in our letters the leaders of all the political clubs and our Congressman and elected representatives, asking them to support us, which they did.

We had only a weekend to mobilize ourselves, and we did it. From every pulpit the parishioners were told what the plans were. The Tenant's Association nearby held an emergency meeting and told their people. The Council held an emergency executive committee meeting and passed the word. Hamilton-Madison House and the local churches held emergency meetings and mobilized people.

The press releases were prepared; volunteers came in and rushed them out special delivery to newspapers and television stations. Our contacts with newspapers and TV people were immediately scanned. Picket signs were drawn up. Flyers, 10,000 flyers, were prepared on a small hand machine on an overnight basis.

Finally the glorious day came which once again put us back into "mania" because we were taking the initiative, we were strong, and on the morning of the 12th of May, at 10:00 o'clock, still having received no word from the City, we picketed.

Now, this is the only point where the lay, indigenous poor, the people who were going to be served by the program, were actually physically and emotionally involved on behalf of the program itself. They were on the picket lines and they knew why.

I cannot tell you, after all the weekend organizational activities, what an incredibly moving sight it was to see. At 9:30, the priests and the ministers met their parishioners out in front of their church, picket signs in hand; and leading them were elders and deacons, acting much like a marine lieutenant taking a hill. There was a mass movement on Madison Street that made you think that a parade was going to take place that day. Parents who had been beaten down, now finally having a chance to speak out with flyers and picket signs and baby carriages. There, on the scene at 10:00 o'clock, the picketing began.

We had approximately 200 people, old and young. One person was so old he could only march around the circle twice and had to rest. Chinese people, Spanish-speaking people, English-speaking people. Negroes and whites. We had ministers, professional people; we had lay people; we had mothers of kids in last year's program, pushing the baby carriages of younger children for whom they didn't have babysitters. It was the most moving sight that I can remember in my experience with the Council.

We had a fairly careful and sophisticated use of mass media and publications; we stuffed the press boxes over at City Hall—I knew this technique from previous work. We sent our releases to all the papers and

TV stations, not regular mail, but spent the extra money to send them special delivery, so that it had an air of importance.

Mrs. D., who lives in Chatham Green and was chairman of our Program Planning Committee, knew an NBC news reporter who also lives in Chatham Green, and used this contact to have him give us TV coverage. I used a contact through my brother, who is an old newspaper man, to get another paper to cover us. Reverend Y. used some of his contacts. And the end was that here the little Two Bridges Neighborhood Council, a converted two-chair barber shop, which runs on a budget of a few hundred dollars a year, had coverage in the *New York Times,* the *World Telegram & Sun,* the *Daily News,* and four neighborhood papers. Coverage that night on Channel 4, NBC TV, featured individual speeches by Reverend Y. and Mrs. D. in a rather moving picture story of our picketing of the Anti-Poverty Board at a time at which the Board was coming under some heavy criticism.

The next morning, when I came to work, I found a telegram from the Anti-Poverty Board, saying that they were eager to speak with us. The phone started ringing like mad; the Deputy Administrative Director of the Anti-Poverty Board wanted to know when they could meet with us; and they were so sorry, and didn't we know they really were very interested in us. Our Congressman was on the phone to us; our Councilman was on the phone; every one wanted to know what they could do.

From that point on, we saw that our new strategy of direct confrontation and conflict was clearly correct: that it was well taken; that our show of strength had been successful; that our planned publicity, and our coordinated picket line, our TV and press coverage, and all of the hundred and one little details that went into it, were sufficient to put the City in an embarrassing position. Were they now going to reject and hold up the Two Bridges Neighborhood Council's proposal, and be further embarrassed by it in a political year, with Mr. Screvane running for office? It was easier, frankly, for them to fund us, even though they weren't perhaps particularly eager to do so.

We had a good report that one very highly placed city official said, (when told that we were going to picket) "To hell with Two Bridges, they won't get a dime." But the tone had changed, the day after our picketing, to: "Give Two Bridges their dime, and get them off our backs." This was what we wanted to do; and this, my friends, could never have been done by co-option and co-optation alone. This could only have been achieved by conflict.

We also had another weapon, and that was that all of the time the federal OEO people were strongly behind us. There wasn't much, frankly, that they could do, because the proposal had to go through city machinery before it could come into their hands. But we had in the back of our minds, that if, after picketing, the City still refused to give in, we might try to see if we could implement a little-known and little-used clause in the federal law which says that in exceptional cases OEO will consider direct submission of neighborhood programs (bypassing the city) if one can prove good cause. Knowing we had federal support, we had this club behind our back, and I have a feeling that the City was equally scared of this club as they were of the 200 neighborhood people who were picketing their office and embarrassing them in an election year.

Finally, the proposal went through the City's two committees. It actually went to Washington on the 11th of June. And when you realize that we submitted our proposal to the City on the 31st of March, you can see what we mean by delays: the City had held this thing up for over two months.

What problems, internally, were we going under all of this time? Well, when we could only tell our teachers (on the 11th of June) that our proposal was then going to Washington, they were being tempted by Head Start monies. Naturally, many of our good teachers left us and said, "Look, we have to earn a living this summer; it's the 11th of June."

I would like to underline the dedicated teachers and the dedicated top administrative staff who did not abandon the ship; who said, "We believe in this program; we believe that it will be funded. We are going to stick it out, right until the very end." This includes people like Mr. K. and Margaret Z., and Pam C. and Harry M., down through the teachers, and the teachers' assistants, who stuck with us. It was a wonderful, inspiring sight, because they had much to lose if we had not been funded.

In order to insure that our program would get prompt federal treatment, we went down to Washington. The chairman of the Neighborhood Council, the chairman of the Program Planning Committee, a local minister, and myself met with the OEO officials there, who assured us that our proposal was probably the best prepared of any proposal in the City. Meanwhile, our Congressman was working strongly on our behalf; and our proposal was going through the mill quickly in Washington. So, on our visit on the 16th of June we came back with no promises, but informal assurances that our proposal would, in fact, be passed, and that probably Mr. Shriver would be sitting down to sign the summer city package sometime that coming weekend.

Then the great moment. On Tuesday, the 22nd of June, our proposal was signed and the issue of the *Two Bridges News* (which we had been holding up to publish when we were assured funding) came out, Wednesday, June 23rd, and was circulated all over the neighborhood, with the news hot off the press that there would be a reading program for 400 youngsters in the neighborhood this summer. And workshops for their parents, and almost every component that we had asked for, with the exception of the eyeglasses and the films.

Question
What were some of the most exciting things in the program itself that made us feel it was so successful?

Answer
First, the workshops. I've never seen trilingual workshops so successful before. Parents, Chinese, English, and Spanish speaking—who had never come to anything before, attended these workshops; attendance of the youngsters themselves was an unprecedented 90 percent. And remember, these are the youngsters who find it the most difficult to attend school, and tend to be the most truant. For the first time we involved Puerto Rican and Chinese immigrant families; teachers who had been disgusted in many ways with the public school system now were excited by a new opportunity to teach on an individualized basis. The new materials we brought in were materials and books that had in the most part never been used in the public and parochial schools before. We began libraries for each youngster in his home; and youngsters, for the first time, were seen sitting on street corners and stoops, reading books for fun. We found out about the parents' feelings about the schools. We convinced the parents, I really believe we convinced them, that their children were not stupid after all.

The 90 percent attendance, the workshops, the involvement for the first time of Puerto Rican and Chinese families, the feedback to the teachers who were excited about what you can do in a small, individualized setting: the tremendous impact on a community that had picketed, that had mobilized itself for something and had won, in fact, won over larger forces. The new materials which we had experimented with; the integrated, urban-oriented books, for example. The home libraries that the children were getting in their homes; the books for the first time that they were excited to read on their own—and at home, and on street corners; the parents feelings about the schools which we had elicited for the first time; the change in the parents' minds—that they no longer regarded their child as stupid, but as a child who, with their help at home, and the teacher's help in school, could in fact make real progress. The thousand people we had at graduation. I don't ever remember a thousand people who are poor: people who are deprived. Finally, all we can say is the reaction of the Eastern Regional Director of the Office of Economic Opportunity who said that he felt the Two Bridges Neighborhood Council's Summer Reading Program was "probably one of the finest programs of its kind anywhere in the country."

Now, I'd like to say just a little bit, briefly, about where we go from here. Others have spoken about the program itself, with far more experience and expertise than I can. But I think the important thing is that the community process not be lost. That what we began to do with these parents be continued; that these parents not be left behind. And we have made plans to insure that this does not happen.

In our proposal, we provided that the senior community coordinator would continue on staff on a part-time basis through the end of December, and she continues to do so, operating out of the Two Bridges Neighborhood Council office. She has compiled all of the records of the youngsters, and is feeding these records and reports back into the public and parochial schools they attend, so that the guidance counselors and the teachers can use this material to better understand and better work with the children in their classes. These folders included individual write-ups each day by the teachers on their children; home visit summaries by community coordinators; and in many cases, diagnostic workups made by a consulting psychologist.

In addition, we are using some of the unexpected funds through the end of December to continue certain research aspects of the program.

We are planning on the basis of our successful parent workshop (and the importance of involving the *parents* in the education of their child) a Parent Development Program proposal, which has now been written —not this time largely by professionals, but by professionals and lay people together. And in the proposal one can see that over 50 percent of the planning committee were laymen, parents of youngsters in the program, and who were people who would well qualify as indigenous and perhaps even as poor.

We are making sure that in this program that we have a board of education of which more than 50 percent must be laymen. And this board will hire and supervise the director of the program. This is not like the situation this summer. Where the director was really not responsible to laymen, and where we did not have a board of directors, and where, therefore, lay participation and lay authority was quite small, and professional authority and participation quite strong. We are clear about the direction in which we intend to move.

My final word would be: How can other communities learn from our experience and mobilize to develop a community action program? What was it, in terms of community organization process and principles that made this program successful?

Questions

1. What role or roles do you see the social worker taking? (In answering the following questions cite the place in which your answer can be found.)
2. What systems do you see operating in the account? List some instances of interdependence and interaction.
3. In the background account, what model of community organization do you see described?
4. How was the planned change process initiated in 1965? Who was the initiator?
5. What were the strengths noted by Kurzman? Strengths of children? Strengths of teachers? Strengths of parents? What other strengths in the program can you see?
6. Analyze the makeup of the neighborhood council. What power did the members have? What power did they have access to?
7. Do you see the neighborhood council as an activist group? Why?
8. Did the council use mainly collaborative or mainly conflict tactics?
9. In this context, what does the term "'laymen" mean?
10. Analyze the potential conflict between the Board of Education and the Education Committee of the Two Bridges Neighborhood Council.
11. Describe the process of proposal writing. Do you think this was the most expeditious way of writing the proposal? What changes would you have made in the process?
12. Can you account for the large numbers of man-hours given by members of the Education Committee?
13. Does the question of funding arise in the context of most community-based social work? How is it usually resolved?
14. Do you feel that social workers should be involved in fund raising?
15. Do you see any connection between casework or group work skills and fund raising?
16. Why was the Board of Education not considered a possibility for funding?
17. In the account of the responsibilities of the social worker, which tasks would you feel able to handle? Which seem too much?
18. Describe the contrast between the climate of feeling at the time of submission of the proposal on March 31 and during the waiting period, which stretched to six weeks.
19. Do you agree with the strategy finally used to get a response from the Anti-Poverty Council? Why?

20. Do you regard the preparation of press releases as part of the social worker's job? Why?
21. What was the effect on the community of the long delay in decision-making? How was the tension used?
22. What was the interrelationship between city and federal government which was crucial to the decision?
23. List some of the components of the program which seem to you to be valuable from a social work view. Which components were educational in their focus?
24. Can you visualize a school social work program growing out of the Two Bridges neighborhood council program? Why? Why not?

Appendix C

The following case study outlines a school social work situation with a nine-year-old boy. Solutions to his problem must be worked out by the reader.

Tommy Edwards*

Tommy Edwards, a nine-year-old Caucasian boy attending fourth grade in a kindergarten through fourth-grade school that covered a district with a wide socioeconomic range, was referred to the school social worker and described as a constant classroom troublemaker. Most of the following information was obtained from the principal.

Although Tommy tested in the average range of intelligence, he had never done well in school. His parents were both deaf and his mother was also mute. She was known to go into rages at neighborhood children and their parents when she thought they were making fun of her or picking on Tommy. She frequently thought Tommy was abused in normal interaction in play and seemed somewhat overprotective and lacking in knowledge of normal childhood development. When she was angry, she waved her arms and made faces in such a manner that the message of rage was clear. Tommy's father worked regularly as a janitor in a local hospital.

---

* This unpublished case material is the property of Dr. Mary Jo Lockwood, Assistant Professor at Florida State University.

Their home, though shabby, was clean and fairly well-kept. The neighborhood, on the edge of an extremely affluent part of town, was run-down, dirty and unkept. Mrs. Edwards was isolated from most normal contacts in the neighborhood. One neighbor occasionally came over for coffee. Mrs. Edwards communicated by lip reading and writing. When she was annoyed with Tommy, she turned her back on him, which cut him off completely.

In school, Tommy was inattentive, read poorly, and did not complete his work. His teacher, a middle-aged woman with a traditional approach, had lost all patience with Tommy. She was merely lasting out the year, after which he would go to another school. She could not imagine Tommy ever fitting into her class. In observing the class, the worker felt that the teacher jumped on Tommy for errors she ignored in others. Tommy responded with stubbornness followed by tantrums and bad language.

The principal had tried several times to establish contact with Tommy's mother. She was unwilling to come to school for conferences and had been angry when the principal had visited. The principal and Tommy had a fairly good relationship. When Tommy was "sent to the office," the principal could calm him down quickly and had found that short periods of isolation were most effective in helping Tommy regain control of himself.

Tommy's father was a rather withdrawn person who seemed to be the dominant partner in the marriage. He and Tommy did very little together. He worked long hours and Mrs. Edwards apparently turned to him for decisions. His hours made him difficult to interview. There was no extended family in town. Mrs. Edwards' sister lived about a hundred miles away.

On the playground, Tommy was observed to play well with two or three other boys. He was well coordinated and enjoyed active play. He sometimes talked by moving his lips only and mispronounced many words. Tommy talked with the social worker casually one day in the office. He mentioned the fact that he badly wanted a dog. He had wanted to play Little League baseball, but had no way to get to the practice field as it was too far to walk and his father was not home by that time. The worker found him friendly.

The Edwards lived in a city of 500,000 with a number of social services. Church-going was an important part of the social life of the city. There was little public transportation. The city had an extensive recreation department and there was a park near the Edwards' with a swimming pool and a summer program. The school system had available psychologists (who usually tested); nurses, speech, reading and hearing consultants; and elementary teaching consultants. There was one class for emotionally disturbed children in the building. This school did not qualify for any special federal programs. There was an organization for the disabled that operated a day program of recreation and crafts and provided bus transportation nearby. Vocational rehabilitation was available through the Department of Welfare. There was a medical school in the city with a variety of outpatient clinics including an excellent children's psychiatric clinic for those children who were interesting teaching cases. There was a private family social service agency with a sliding fee scale.

Questions

1. Whom would you interview first? Why?
2. How would you begin?
3. Do you think you need all the background information? Why?
4. What kinds of feelings do you have about Tommy's mother? What kinds of feelings do you think the principal has about her?
5. What additional information do you need? Where would you get it?
6. With whom would you try to make contacts and for what purpose? List as many as you can, in order of priority.
7. What principles of relationship can you see applying to Tommy? To the principal of the school? To Tommy's mother?
8. As a school social worker, what would be your responsibility to your own agency? To the school? To Tommy?
9. What other agencies would you consider involving in this case?
10. As the school social worker involved, try writing a report on this case, beginning with the referral from the teacher. Use a planned change outline which will show the beginning, middle, and end of the case. Choose either a satisfactory or unsatisfactory solution but make clear the reasons for the outcome of the case.

Selected bibliography*

CHAPTER 1

Bartlett, Harriett M., *The Common Base of Social Work Practice.* National Association of Social Workers, N.Y., 1970.

——————, "Toward Clarification and Improvement of Social Work Practice—A Working Definition of Social Work Practice," *Social Work,* vol. 3, no. 2 (1958), p. 3. An analysis of trends and issues in the thinking about social work practice.

Collins, Alice H., *The Human Services: An Introduction.* The Odyssey Press, Indianapolis and N.Y., 1973. Describes the tasks needed by human service workers and discusses the skills necessary to carry out these tasks.

Crampton, Helen M. and Kaiser, Kenneth K., *Social Welfare: Institution and Process.* Random House, N.Y., 1970. An easy-to-read, historical and case study view of social welfare in the United States.

Fink, Arthur E., *The Field of Social Work.* Holt, Rinehart and Winston, N.Y., 1974, 6th ed. A classic text which includes history, fields of practice, methods, and many case studies.

Friedlander, Walter, and Apte, Robert, ed., *Introduction to Social Welfare: Concepts and Methods in Social Work.* Englewood Cliffs, N.J., Prentice Hall, 1974, 6th ed. A comprehensive text covering nearly all aspects of social welfare and social work.

Gordon, William E., "A Critique of the Working Definition," *Social Work,* vol. 7, no. 4 (1962), p. 3. An article which expands, enlarges and discusses the working definition proposed by Bartlett.

Klenk, Robert W., and Ryan, Robert M., ed., *The Practice of Social Work.* Wadsworth, Belmont, Ca., 1974, 2d ed. A book of readings by many well-known authors, using the social systems approach.

*Works cited in the chapter are not included in this bibliography.

Miller, Henry, "Value Dilemmas in Social Casework," *Social Work,* vol. 13 (January, 1968), p. 27. An article describing the kinds and degrees of dilemmas faced by social workers and their values.

Tripodi, Tony; Fellin, Phillip; Epstein, Irvin; and Lind, Roger, *Social Workers at Work: An Introduction to Social Work Practice.* F. E. Peacock, Itasca, Il., 1972. A book of readings in the methods of casework, group work and community work, with a section dealing with the profession of social work.

CHAPTER 2

Bennis, Warren G., Beune, Kenneth D., and Chin, Robert, ed., *The Planning of Change.* Holt, Rinehart and Winston, N.Y., 1969. A comprehensive book of readings covering planned change theory, systems theory, and strategies for implementation.

Berrien, T. Kenneth, *General and Social Systems.* Rutgers University Press, New Brunswick, N.J., 1968. Applies general systems theory to problems in social psychology without dehumanizing those problems.

Boulding, Kenneth, "General Systems Theory, A Skeleton of Science," *Management Science,* 12 (1956), 197. Outlines the general concepts required to view all areas of life systemically.

Hartman, Ann, "To Think About the Unthinkable," *Social Casework,* vol. 51 (October 1970), p. 467. A simply written article relating social work practice to systems theory.

Janchill, Sister Mary Paul, "Systems Concepts in Casework Theory and Practice," *Social Casework,* vol. 50 (February 1969), p. 74. An article which describes and defines systems theory terms in language familiar to social workers.

Hearn, Gordon, ed., *The General Systems Approach: Contributions Toward an Holistic Conception of Social Work.* Council on Social Work Education, N.Y., 1969. Promotes the development of a substantially inclusive, internally consistent and organized conception of social work practice and its approach to the human scene.

Parsons, Talcott, *The Social System.* The Free Press, Glencoe, Il., 1951. A classic in social systems theory as an application of general systems theory.

Von Bertalanffy, Ludwig, "An Outline of General Systems Theory," *British Journal for the Philosophy of Science,* vol. 1 (1950), p. 134. A biological theory that provided the impetus for general systems theory.

CHAPTER 3

Abbott, Edith, *Some American Pioneers in Social Welfare.* University of Chicago Press, Chicago, 1937. Biographical sketches of some important early social workers in the United States.

Abbott, Grace, *The Child and the State.* University of Chicago Press, Chicago, 1938. An early account of welfare programs for children.

Addams, Jane, *Twenty Years at Hull House*. Macmillan, N.Y., 1910. Miss Addams' own account of early days in the settlement movement in Chicago.

Beers, Clifford, *A Mind that Found Itself*. Doubleday, N.Y., 1935. A firsthand account of institutional care for the mentally ill in the first part of the century.

Breckenridge, Sophonisba P., *Public Welfare Administration in the United States*, 3rd impression. University of Chicago Press, Chicago, 1935. A classic account of the United States' early efforts at welfare administration.

Harrington, Michael, *The Other America*. Penguin Books, Baltimore, Maryland, 1962. Reputed to be the book that sparked the war on poverty, it details some of the kinds of poverty to be found in the most affluent country in the world.

Kincaid, J. C., *Poverty and Equality in Britain*. Penguin Books, Middlesex, England, 1973. A recent book which explodes the theory that Britain has solved the poverty problem.

CHAPTER 4

Cohen, Ruth, "Outreach and Advocacy in the Treatment of the Aged," *Social Casework*, vol. 55 (May 1974), p. 271. An article describing three projects which demonstrate the value of maintaining older persons in the mainstream of community life. The methods of intervention include outreach and advocacy.

Fox, Evelyn, et al., "The Termination Process: A Neglected Dimension in Social Work," *Social Work*, vol. 14 (October 1969), p. 53. An article which discusses relevant theory, the reasons for termination, and an extensive clinical example of a 12-year-old girl, based on observations through a one-way mirror during five therapy sessions, to point up the important aspects of the process, the client's feelings, and the worker's problems in helping the client work through termination.

Garrett, Annette, *Interviewing: Its Principles and Methods*. Family Service Association of America, N.Y. 1943. A classic book on social work interviewing, particularly for casework interviews.

Glasser, William, *Reality Therapy*. Harper and Row, N.Y. 1965. Glasser's book describes the theory and practice of dealing with juveniles in the here and now, without excuses. He explains the importance of personal involvement by the worker.

Kadushin, Alfred, *Child Welfare Services: A Sourcebook*. Crowell-Collier and Macmillan, N.Y., 1970. A thorough and comprehensive book which describes the kinds and quality of services which have been offered to children in this country.

Kaufman, Irving, M.D., "Helping People Who Cannot Manage Their Lives," *Children*, vol. 13, (May–June 1966), p. 93. A psychiatrist discusses the kinds of character disorders which call for intervention outside the classic intrapsychic methods of treatment. He uses the term "emotionally retarded," and suggests the implications of treating such people.

Oxley, Genevieve, "The Caseworkers Expectation and Client Motivation," *Social Casework*, vol. 47 (July 1966), p. 432. An article which discusses the effect of positive and negative expectation by the caseworker on the role of the client in the casework process.

Scheunemann, Yolanda, and French, Betty, "Diagnosis as the Foundation of Professional Service," *Social Casework*, vol. 55 (March 1974), p. 135. An article which categorizes and describes the kinds of assessment which can be made after one or two interviews to plan treatment and length of contract.

Shubert, Margaret, *Interviewing in Social Work Practice: An Introduction.* Council on Social Work Education, N.Y., 1971. An up-to-date book enumerating factors affecting the interview, common types of interviews, and the dimensions which must be taken into account.

Smalley, Ruth, *Theory for Social Work Practice.* Columbia University Press, N.Y. and London, 1967. A textbook which outlines a common base for social work practice whether with individuals, groups or communities.

Szasz, Thomas, *The Myth of Mental Illness.* Harper and Row, N.Y., 1961. One of the first of many books which question the medical basis of mental illness, and posit the theory that illness and health are matters of opinion rather than fact.

CHAPTER 5

Ackerman, Nathan W., *Treating the Troubled Family.* Basic Books, N.Y., 1966. A book written by an acknowledged authority in the field of family therapy. The author discusses assessment, planning and treatment from a systems orientation.

Billingsley, Andrew, *Black Families in White America.* Prentice Hall, Englewood Cliffs, N.J., 1968. A book giving a black perspective on families and how they live in this country.

Bracy, John J. et al., *Black Matriarchy: Myth or Reality.* Wadsworth, Belmont, Ca., 1970. A book which disputes the stereotype of black culture as a matriarchy.

Hartman, Ann, "The Generic Stance and the Family Agency," *Social Casework*, vol. 55 (April 1974), p. 170. An article which expands the idea of an extended model of action, so that the client and all related systems are included.

Satir, Virginia, *Conjoint Family Therapy.* Science and Behavior Press, Palo Alto, Ca., 1967. A book written in very simple, easily understood form, describing communicative family therapy.

Younghusband, Eileen, ed., *Social Casework with Families.* University of Chicago Press, Chicago, 1965. A book of articles by U.S. and English authors, describing some kinds of work done in family settings by workers who see themselves as caseworkers.

CHAPTER 6

Cartwright, Dorwin and Zander, Alvin, ed., *Group Dynamics, Research and Theory*. Row, Peterson, Evanston, Il., 1953. The "bible" of group dynamics; a large and comprehensive reference.

Garland, James A., Jones, Hubert, and Kolodny, Ralph, "A Model for Stages in the Development of Social Work Groups." In Saul Berstein, ed., *Explorations of Groupwork*. Boston University Press, Boston, 1965. A simple, easily understood model for group development and process.

Hartford, Margaret, *Groups in Social Work*. Columbia University Press, N.Y. and London, 1972. An application of small group theory and research to social work practice.

Lewis, Howard and Sheffield, Harold, *Growth Games*. Bantam Books, N.Y., 1970. Some practical how-to exercises in growth groups.

Northen, Helen, *Social Work with Groups*. Columbia University Press, N.Y. and London, 1969. A systems-oriented explanation of social group work for the beginning practitioner.

Thomas, Edwin J., ed., *Behavioral Science for Social Workers*. Free Press, N.Y., 1967. A collection of readings in various areas of social work, including group work.

CHAPTER 7

Alinsky, Saul, *Reveille for Radicals*. University of Chicago Press, Chicago, 1946. Alinsky's philosophy as he expressed it in 1946.

Clark, Kenneth, *Dark Ghetto: Dilemmas of Social Power*. Harper and Row, N.Y., 1965. The view of power from a black perspective.

Cox, Fred, et al., *Strategies of Community Organization*. F. E. Peacock, Itasca, Il., 1970. A book of readings discussing definitions, variations, strategies, and linkages.

Dunham, Arthur, *Community Welfare Organization, Principles and Practice*. Thomas Crowell, N.Y., 1958. A traditional explanation of locality development as viewed by early community workers.

Kramer, Ralph, and Specht, Harry, *Readings in Community Organization Practice*. Prentice Hall, Englewood Cliffs, N.J., 1969. A book of readings discussing the context and process of community work in terms of analysis, problem-solving, roles, and social planning.

Ross, Murray, *Case Histories in Community Organization*. Harper and Row, N.Y., 1958. A casebook of community organization problems with questions to be answered at the end of each chapter.

Shaffer, Anatole, "Community Organization and the Oppressed," *Journal of Education for Social Work*, vol. 8 (Fall 1972), p. 65. An article explaining the dilemma of working for the oppressed while a member of the oppressor group.

Index